Student Companion to

Charlotte
&Emily
BRONTË

Student Companion to

Charlotte & Emily BRONTË

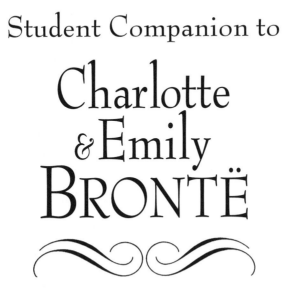

Barbara Z. Thaden

Student Companions to Classic Writers

Greenwood Press
Westport, Connecticut • London

Library of Congress Cataloging-in-Publication Data

Thaden, Barbara, 1955–
    Student companion to Charlotte and Emily Brontë / Barbara Z. Thaden.
        p.   cm.—(Student companions to classic writers, ISSN 1522–7979)
    Includes bibliographical references (p.   ) and index.
    ISBN 0–313–31053–X (alk. paper)
        1. Brontë, Charlotte, 1816–1855—Criticism and interpretation.   2. Women and
literature—England—History—19th century.   3. Brontë, Emily, 1818–1848—
Criticism and interpretation.   4. Brontë, Charlotte, 1816–1855—Examinations—
Study guides.   5. Brontë, Emily, 1818–1848—Examinations—Study guides.
    6. Brontë, Charlotte, 1816–1855—Handbooks, manuals, etc.   7. Brontë, Emily,
1818–1848—Handbooks, manuals, etc.   I. Title.   II. Series.
    PR4169.T46   2001
    823′.809—dc21   00–052133

British Library Cataloguing in Publication Data is available.

Library of Congress Catalog Card Number: 00–052133
ISBN: 0–313–31053–X
ISSN: 1522–7979

First published in 2001

Greenwood Press, 88 Post Road West, Westport, CT 06881
An imprint of Greenwood Publishing Group, Inc.
www.greenwood.com

Printed in the United States of America

The paper used in this book complies with the
Permanent Paper Standard issued by the National
Information Standards Organization (Z39.48–1984).

10 9 8 7 6 5 4 3 2 1

Contents

Series Foreword

This series has been designed to meet the needs of students and general readers for accessible literary criticism on the American and world writers most frequently studied and read in the secondary school, community college, and four-year college classrooms. Unlike other works of literary criticism that are written for the specialist and graduate student, or that feature a variety of reprinted scholarly essays on sometimes obscure aspects of the writer's work, the Student Companions to Classic Writers series is carefully crafted to examine each writer's major works fully and in a systematic way, at the level of the nonspecialist and general reader. The objective is to enable the reader to gain a deeper understanding of the work and to apply critical thinking skills to the act of reading. The proven format for the volumes in this series was developed by an advisory board of teachers and librarians for a successful series published by Greenwood Press, Critical Companions to Popular Contemporary Writers. Responding to their request for easy-to-use and yet challenging literary criticism for students and adult library patrons, Greenwood Press developed a systematic format that is not intimidating but helps the reader to develop the ability to analyze literature.

How does this work? Each volume in the Student Companions to Classic Writers series is written by a subject specialist, an academic who understands students' needs for basic and yet challenging examination of the writer's canon. Each volume begins with a biographical chapter, drawn from published sources, biographies, and autobiographies, that relates the writer's life to his or her work. The next chapter examines the writer's literary heritage, tracing the literary influences of other writers on that writer and explaining and discussing the literary genres into which the writer's work falls. Each of the following chapters examines a major work by the writer, those works most frequently read and studied by high school and college students. Depending on the writer's canon, generally between four and eight major works are examined, each in an individual chapter. The discussion of each work is organized into separate sections on plot development, character development, and major themes. Literary devices and style, narrative point of view, and historical setting are also discussed in turn if pertinent to the work. Each chapter concludes with an alternate critical perspective from which to read the work, such as a psychological or feminist criticism. The critical theory is defined briefly in easy, comprehensible language for the student. Looking at the literature from the point of view of a particular critical approach will help the reader to understand and apply critical theory to the act of reading and analyzing literature.

Of particular value in each volume is the bibliography, which includes a complete bibliography of the writer's works, a selected bibliography of biographical and critical works suitable for students, and lists of reviews of each work examined in the companion, all of which will be helpful to readers, teachers, and librarians who would like to consult additional sources.

As a source of literary criticism for the student or for the general reader, this series will help the reader to gain understanding of the writer's work and skill in critical reading.

Preface

The *Student Companion to Charlotte and Emily Brontë* is designed for students and teachers who need a systematic overview of the Brontë novels. Because Emily Brontë wrote only one novel, *Wuthering Heights*, she shares a volume with her more prolific older sister, Charlotte. Charlotte Brontë's best-known novel, *Jane Eyre*, should not completely overshadow her other masterworks, *Shirley* and *Villette*. *The Professor*, Charlotte's first novel, was not published until after her death, and therefore its chapter appears last. Although rarely taught, *The Professor* is important in presenting some of the major themes that appear in all of Charlotte's novels.

This *Companion* provides an introduction to the characteristics of each novel with occasional references to some of the major critics, whose works are listed in the bibliography. A short biographical chapter highlights the familial and personal influences on the Brontë sisters, such as their brother Branwell's emotional and moral collapse and their experience as students and teachers in a Belgian school.

Chapter 2 explains some key concepts in the history of the English novel. For example, are the Brontës "Romantic" or "Victorian," and what do those terms mean anyway? Do their novels fit into one or more of the genre categories such as bildungsroman, domestic fiction, spiritual autobiography, or realistic fiction? How were the Brontës influenced by the Romantic poets, especially Wordsworth and Byron? What is a Byronic hero? What themes recur in all or many of the novels? How did the Brontës influence the development of the novel as a genre? Because I use *Jane Eyre* and *Wuthering Heights* to help explain some of these concepts, readers are encouraged to re-read this chapter after reading one or both of these novels.

The remaining chapters are each devoted to a single novel. The first section of each not only describes what happens in each novel but also explains how the plot is structured. Then each major character is described and discussed as either a round character—one who changes and matures—or as a flat character, who does not change. The section on "Thematic Issues" identifies, explains, and clarifies such themes as patriarchal oppression, the imprisoning nature of marriage for women, orphanhood and homelessness, and the problem of being a middle-class unmarried woman. While each novel will have some unique themes, many of them share the same themes, so a student can consult the "Thematic Issues" section of all the chapters for help on understanding certain themes in any of the novels. Similarly, many of the novels share "Historical/Social Cultural Contexts," so readers can benefit from skimming this section of each chapter. For example, both *The Professor* and *Villette* take place in Belgium, so they share many of the same historical and cultural contexts, and students who are studying *Villette* can benefit by reading the chapter on *The Professor* as well.

The section titled "Literary Devices and Craft" discusses the use of point of view, symbolism, allusion, imagery, extended or central metaphors, pairing of characters and settings, personification, irony, and other literary devices. Readers can benefit by reviewing this section of each chapter as well, since Charlotte often used the same literary devices in very similar ways. The discussion of each novel ends with an analysis using a contemporary critical approach, such as Freudian, Jungian, Feminist, Marxist, and Postcolonial literary theory. Students can read this section on each novel and try applying different critical approaches to different novels.

I wish to thank Dr. Michele Ware of North Carolina Central University for reading and editing each chapter, for identifying places in the manuscript where high school and college students might need additional clarification, and for her friendship and support. I also wish to thank The United Negro College Fund for its generous award of the Henry C. McBay Research Fellowship, which allowed me to take a semester's leave of absence, without which this project could not have been completed. I thank the administration of St. Augustine's College in Raleigh for granting me generous release time, and my colleagues for their enthusiastic support. My editor at Greenwood Press, Ms. Lynn Malloy, was extremely helpful in offering not only sound editorial advice but also positive feedback when I needed it most. I owe the greatest thanks, however, to my husband, David Thaden, for his never failing emotional, moral, and spiritual support, and to my sons Michael and Matthew for their patience and love.

1

An Extraordinary Family

Although Charlotte and Emily Brontë's novels have been extremely popular ever since their publication, the uniquely intense, personal, and tragically short lives of the authors have attracted just as much interest and attention. Charlotte was the third and Emily the fifth of six children born to Patrick Brontë, a Church of England clergyman who had immigrated to England from Ireland, and Maria Branwell, an English girl he married in 1812.

From this union sprang one of the most extraordinarily gifted literary families in the history of literature. Maria Branwell's six children, five of whom were born in the village of Bradford, Yorkshire, were all unusually precocious. However, only one year after giving birth to her youngest child, and only eighteen months after moving to the nearby village of Haworth, where Patrick would remain for the rest of his life, Maria Branwell, who seems to have had ovarian cancer, was dead.

Thus, in 1821, Patrick Brontë found himself a widower with six young children: Maria; Elizabeth; Charlotte (born April 21, 1816); Branwell, the only son; Emily (born July 30, 1818); and Anne. Patrick was busy with his clerical duties and considered children more of a nuisance than a pleasure. When his halfhearted attempts to attract a second wife to care for his brood failed, he convinced his deceased wife's older unmarried sister, Elizabeth Branwell, to keep house for him.

Left to their own resources from infancy, the Brontë children formed deep emotional bonds with each other. Growing up motherless, isolated, and with minimal contact with their father, who educated them at home but did not even take his meals with them, they created a world of the imagination that was far more real to them than any outside world could ever be. Raised in spartan simplicity, less because of poverty than because of their father's strict religious principles, they found excitement and novelty in a world of ideas, not things. Patrick Brontë was so intent on not spoiling his children that they reportedly were given no meat to eat and never allowed to wear fancy clothes, even though the Brontës could probably afford both. Patrick Brontë was of the evangelical strain of Anglicanism. While high church Anglicanism looked to the splendors and ceremonies of the Roman Catholic Church as its model, the evangelical or low church movement rebelled against the worldliness and political intrigues of both the Roman Catholic and Anglican church. Rather than ceremony and blind obedience to custom, the evangelicals believed in man's sinfulness and need for redemption through a personal communion with God enabled by studying the infallible Holy Scripture.

Haworth parish, although well known for evangelicanism, was also known for its wild, rough "heathen" ways. Most inhabitants worked in the manufacture of wool. There were no child-labor laws, so young children also worked long hours in the mills. Patrick Brontë did not want his children associating with the children of factory workers, because he was an educated man, although a poor one. He had what we would call a "white-collar" job and hoped his children would enjoy the same type of life, if not better. His children could have nothing in common with illiterate, dirty, unsupervised children born only to labor and die.

The Brontë children were therefore a world unto themselves, never visiting or being visited by other children, since they were the only educated family in the isolated village. Aunt Branwell served as housekeeper and surrogate mother. Although she probably loved the children, she was authoritarian and not overtly affectionate. Two years after her arrival, Patrick Brontë heard of a new school at Cowan Bridge for the daughters of poor clergymen and felt that this was an opportunity to educate his daughters.

The Clergy Daughter's School was a charity institution founded by a wealthy clergyman named William Carus Wilson. Both school and founder have found perpetual infamy as Lowood School and the Reverend Brocklehurst in Charlotte's first published novel, *Jane Eyre*. Patrick packed off his two oldest girls, Maria and Elizabeth, then only ten and nine years old, little suspecting that he was sending them to their deaths. Maria and Elizabeth arrived in July 1824. Patrick sent Charlotte and Emily to join them later that year. Emily, barely six, was the youngest child ever enrolled at the school.

The food at Cowan Bridge School was inedible. The slovenly cook prepared rotten meats, cooked in rancid fat, and boiled foods in dirty water collected from the rain tub. The younger girls—and the Brontë children were among the youngest at the school—lived in semi-starvation, as any edible food was often snatched from them by the older, even more ravenous girls. Some teachers were cruel, but the founder of the school reminded his pupils that severe discipline, cold, and hunger were good for the souls of charity children. In addition, the school was situated in an unhealthy area, and poor sanitary conditions contributed to illness and infection. The entire school suffered a typhus epidemic, but Maria and Elizabeth both contracted tuberculosis. Charlotte watched her oldest sister abused and mistreated and both her older sisters decline in health. Less than seven months after sending his oldest daughters, Patrick was informed that Maria was ill but arrived to find her near death. Maria died in the spring of 1825, and Elizabeth died that summer. Charlotte and Emily were removed from the school, but Charlotte would never forget the horrors she experienced there; her sister Maria has been immortalized as the angelic Helen Burns in *Jane Eyre*.

Charlotte was now the oldest of the four remaining children, who again retreated into their compelling fantasy world. They wrote many pages of manuscript chronicling the histories of several imaginary kingdoms. Their characters lived fantastical, passionate, romantic, immoral, violent, and evil lives. At first all the children wrote about Glasstown, in Angria, an imaginary kingdom in Africa. Later, Emily and Anne would concentrate on the kingdom of Gondol, while Charlotte and Branwell continued the Glasstown Chronicles.

Charlotte was again sent away to school in 1831, to Roe Head. She was considered odd, with her tiny "undeveloped" figure (which she attributed to undernourishment at Cowan Bridge), her old-fashioned clothing, and her extreme nearsightedness. But she won the respect of the other girls by her studiousness and integrity. In 1835, Charlotte returned to Roe Head as a teacher, taking Emily with her as a pupil. While Charlotte was tiny, Emily was tall and gangly; while Charlotte was shy, Emily was "reserved," meaning that it appeared to everyone that she did not care to speak to them. Charlotte was miserable because her teaching duties took her away from her writing, but Emily was miserable because she was not at home. She was expected to behave in a ladylike way, to follow a schedule, to rein in her imagination, and this she could not do without letting her body die with her spirit. "Liberty was the breath of Emily's nostrils. The change from her own home to a school, from her own noiseless, very secluded, but unrestricted and inartificial mode of life, to one of disciplined routine . . . was what she failed in enduring . . . I felt in my heart she would die, if she did not go home," Charlotte wrote in her "Memoir of Ellis Bell," the prefix to the 1850 edition of her *Poems* (Gerin 95).

Emily was allowed to return home after only three months. A brilliant but uncommunicative and inward girl, she never thrived except when living at home, taking long walks on the heath and enjoying the companionship of her dogs more than that of any person. Charlotte continued as teacher at Roe Head until 1838. Then all three sisters went out as teachers to various posts. Charlotte took a position as governess, which she hated. Emily took a position as teacher, which she found even more dreadful. Over a Christmas break, the sisters hatched the plan of opening their own school. To prepare themselves, Charlotte and Emily planned to further their own education in Europe, while Anne was to take care of their aging and almost blind father.

In 1842, Charlotte and Emily left for Brussels, Belgium, to study French and German, and to teach English and music, at the Pensionnat Heger, a girls' boarding and day school. Charlotte was well liked by her students, although she seems hardly to have realized it. Emily was hated. The students made fun of her old-fashioned clothes, her refusal to engage in conversation, and her apparent unconcern for their happiness. M. Heger found her unfeminine and said that she should have been a man. Emily never spoke, even when spoken to, unless the topic was one she felt strongly about, and then she would defend her point in a most unfeminine manner. The sisters were rarely invited out because if Charlotte was invited, Emily must come also, even though she would sit like a stone the entire evening and make everyone uncomfortable.

After a year in Brussels, Emily returned to Haworth and never again left it. But Charlotte was experiencing the great passion of her life; she had fallen deeply—spiritually and emotionally—in love with a professor at the Pensionnat, M. Heger. Married to the headmistress of the Pensionnat Heger, M. Heger was a professor at a distinguished school for boys but also taught at his wife's school for girls. Charlotte convinced herself that another year of study would benefit her, not daring to admit that it was her love for M. Heger that drew her back. He was the most intellectually stimulating man she would ever meet. More than her equal, he was her "master," as she would always refer to him, and this word meant much more than "teacher" to Charlotte. Charlotte could never admit even to herself the depth and desperation of her passion, for M. Heger was a happily married man and the father of a large and growing family. Madame Heger, however, saw the truth and began to make sure the two were never alone. Charlotte felt as if a soul mate were being torn from her. Her loneliness and despair form the emotional background to her last novel, *Villette*. Convinced that Madame Heger hated her for no reason, Charlotte barely endured her second year in Brussels. She hoped to continue a lifelong correspondence with M. Heger, but as his wife was also his secretary and because M. Heger must have suspected that Charlotte's devotion to him went beyond a student-professor infatuation, his letters soon ceased.

Meanwhile, Emily had found a deep source of life and strength in her own imagination. She had begun writing poetry while living unmolested by social conventions and expectations at Haworth. The loves of her life were her animals—dogs, cats, and even a falcon—and the heath-covered moors around her home. She was strong and brave—the villagers describe how she once single-handedly broke up a vicious dogfight—yet at the same time unworldly, totally uninterested in society outside her own family.

The sisters' plan to start a school was prevented by their brother's living at home. Branwell, disappointed in his professional aspirations, was fast becoming an alcoholic, and his conduct was so blatantly immoral and out of control that a girls' boarding school at Haworth Parsonage was out of the question. Charlotte's deep depression was only lifted when she accidentally discovered a batch of Emily's poetry and insisted that they try to publish a volume of poems.

Emily was outraged at the invasion of her privacy but eventually agreed to contribute to the publication. The sisters invented the pen names they would use all their lives—Currer Bell and Ellis Bell were Charlotte and Emily's pseudonyms. Charlotte believed that their work would be more fairly judged if they were thought to be male, and Emily wanted absolutely no invasion of her sacred privacy.

The collection of poems, published in May 1846, sold only two copies, but their success in having it published pushed each sister to finish the novel she had been working on. They now hoped they could earn their living through novel writing, as Branwell had been fired from his last post as tutor for carrying on an affair with his employer's wife and was now determined to drink and drug himself to death. He abused opium (then obtainable at pharmacies) and drank himself into insanity. Patrick Brontë did everything in his power to prevent Branwell's self-destruction, even locking the young man into his own bedroom at night to prevent him from setting the house on fire, but all efforts proved futile and he was unable to save his son. Like many nineteenth-century fathers, he had much less interest in or interaction with his daughters, who were left to their own devices.

Branwell's insanity made it even more painfully clear to the Brontë sisters that they would be forced to support themselves if they did not marry. Patrick Brontë was perpetual curate at Haworth, but the rectory would pass on to the next curate after his death, and his salary was too low to provide any type of dowry or inheritance.

These educated daughters of a poor man were in an unfortunate position in nineteenth-century England. It was out of the question that they work as factory hands, milkmaids, servants, farm laborers, washerwomen, or the other employments of working and lower-class women. They were not raised to endure hard physical work, nor to think of themselves as belonging to this class of laborers. The primary occupation of a lady in any station of life above the working class was finding a suitable husband who could support her. For this occupation, however, Charlotte and Emily were unsuited. Neither could bring any money into a marriage. In addition, Charlotte was unattractive, extremely shy, and would not consider marrying anyone she was not in love with; Emily was pathologically unsocial and unable to endure any life other than her solitary one in her father's house. An unmarried woman could work as a governess or a teacher, both abhorrent occupations to both sisters. The only other genteel way of earning a living was to write novels.

Soon the sisters began sending out theirs. Emily's *Wuthering Heights* was accepted first, although not published first, while Charlotte's *The Professor* was rejected. But Charlotte found a different publisher for a second novel that she had completed, *Jane Eyre*. Published in October 1847, *Jane Eyre* was highly acclaimed and became an immediate best-seller. The publisher of *Wuthering Heights* then rushed that novel into print a month later, hoping to profit on the success of the first "Bell" novel. *Wuthering Heights* was also critically acclaimed. Readers sensed the author's great talent and ability but were troubled by the strange, brutal, and coarse nature of the novel.

Before the sisters could begin to enjoy their new literary success, their brother Branwell died unexpectedly in September 1848. No sooner was he buried than Emily, who had caught a cold at his funeral, rapidly declined with what we would call "galloping consumption" or tuberculosis. Her breathing became difficult, her lungs hurt, but she refused to see a doctor or even to acknowledge that she was ill. Like a sick animal, she wanted only to be left alone and to pursue her accustomed duties without interference. Finally, after months of stoically endured agony, Emily agreed to see a doctor—but by that same afternoon she was dead, "turning her face reluctantly from the beautiful sun," as Charlotte wrote.

Emily had died on December 19, 1848, at the age of thirty. Only five months later, Anne followed her to the grave, a victim of the same disease. Charlotte, the last remaining sibling, was devastated. To keep from succumbing completely to despair, she finished her third novel, *Shirley*, which was published in 1849. Although by now a famous author, Charlotte found no pleasure in London society and preferred to remain alone, with her father, at Haworth.

Several years later, she returned to the subject matter of her Brussels experience and wrote her fourth novel, *Villette*, published in 1853. It is a dark tale of agonized love and unbearable loneliness. And Charlotte was lonely. Over the years she had rejected several proposals of marriage, because she had felt that her various suitors were not the soul mate she craved. She did not feel for them as she had felt for M. Heger. Love for Charlotte had to be overwhelmingly passionate and earthshaking, the fortuitous meeting of two like souls and minds, like the two halves of Plato's first human being finding each other (or like Catherine and Heathcliff, although Charlotte thought they were too coarse).

Less than a month after sending *Villette* off to her publisher in 1851, Charlotte again received an unexpected offer of marriage—from her father's assistant curate. Arthur Bell Nichols had worked for Patrick Brontë since 1845. He had known the family through the tragic deaths of Branwell, Emily, and Anne. He had grown passionately in love with Charlotte and felt that he could make her happy. She did not love him, but she was taken aback at the intensity of his love for her. Patrick Brontë, who felt that Charlotte should not marry anyone because of her tiny frame and ill health, was infuriated at the thought of his now famous daughter marrying his lowly assistant curate. His permission to the union was vehemently and contemptuously denied, and Nichols turned in his resignation before Mr. Brontë could dismiss him.

Charlotte could not help but notice Nichols's deepening depression as he waited for his replacement to arrive at Haworth, and she recognized the condition. She slowly came to believe in the depth and honesty of his affection. When he reached his new post, Nichols persuaded Charlotte to correspond with him and then to see him. Patrick Brontë at last relented (he wanted Nichols back as curate, as his replacement had proven most unsatisfactory), and Charlotte married Nichols on June 29, 1854.

Charlotte was thirty-eight years old when she married. Although Nichols was not her intellectual or spiritual soul mate, Charlotte's happiness grew daily. But symptoms of consumption returned, and she became even more ill, probably as a result of pregnancy. Just nine months after her marriage, on March 31, 1855, Charlotte died, and her unborn child could not be saved.

Patrick Brontë, who had survived his wife and all six of his children, set up a very uneasy household with the once despised curate, Arthur Bell Nichols. That same year, Elizabeth Gaskell, Charlotte's friend and also an accomplished and popular novelist, began writing *The Life of Charlotte Brontë*, one of the greatest literary biographies of all time. Mrs. Gaskell convinced Nichols to release the manuscript of Charlotte's first novel, *The Professor*, which was finally published in 1857. Haworth, where Charlotte and Emily spent the better part of their lives, became a shrine, and it remains so today. Brontë fans from all over the world visit it yearly, to walk the heath-covered moors Emily loved, to explore the parsonage, surrounded on three sides by a graveyard, and to explore the countryside that nurtured two of the world's most beloved and renowned authors.

The Brontës and the Novel

The nineteenth century was the great age of the novel, and both Charlotte and Emily Brontë greatly influenced the novel's future development. The Brontës themselves were influenced by the Romantic movement, and Emily's greatest achievement was to infuse the novel form with the lyric intensity and the spiritual, transcendental quality of romantic poetry. Charlotte's greatest contribution was to move the novel form away from its emphasis on plot and towards a detailed exploration of the workings of the human mind.

ROMANTIC OR VICTORIAN?

Jane Eyre and *Wuthering Heights* are more Romantic than Victorian novels, even though both were written during what we call the Victorian period. Charlotte and Emily were both great admirers of the Romantic poets, especially Wordsworth and Byron. When *The Professor* was rejected by publishers for being too prosaic, Charlotte turned back to her Romantic roots and her juvenile Angrian fantasy world to infuse her next novel with more romantic and gothic elements. "The Chronicles of Angria," a long series of narratives written by Charlotte and her brother Branwell, followed the passionate, immoral, larger than life exploits of kings and queens, tyrants and revolutionaries, in an imaginary African kingdom. Romantic fiction is highly charged, emotionally unrestrained, and very personal, as contrasted to the earlier neoclassical ideal of balance, temperance, and urbanity, and the later Victorian realism and naturalism. However, Charlotte was also an important shaper of the most salient characteristics of the Victorian novel: a sense of moral earnestness, a questioning of received truths, and a concern with the inner workings of the human mind.

Romantic writers saw society not as an improvement over savagery, as the neo-classical eighteenth-century writers had, but as a hypocritical prison house of inauthenticity, where people are yoked to rules and customs. Romantics valued the individual's rights over society's needs, and they often celebrated the iconoclast and the heroic rebel. The heroic rebel is also called the Romantic hero. He is a character like or modeled after Prometheus, Napoleon, Milton's Satan, Don Juan, or Cain, who rebels against cosmic or social injustice or tyranny. The rebellion is often hopeless, yet the act of rebelling is seen as heroic. In *Wuthering Heights*, Heathcliff rebels against all the laws of God and man, but because he is motivated by a great love that transcends all laws, he is often seen as heroic. In *Jane Eyre*, Rochester rebels against the laws of marriage, which prevent him from divorcing Bertha, by claiming that the laws themselves are unjust and arbitrary. He feels morally justified in asking Jane to be his wife or mistress, because he has divorced himself from Bertha, whether or not the laws of God and man permit or acknowledge that divorce.

Many critics see in Rochester and Heathcliff the typical "Byronic hero." The Byronic hero (the hero of all Byron's poems, which were autobiographical at the same time they were highly romantic) is a "romantic" hero because of his passion, his amorality, his iconoclasm, his homelessness, and his desperation. He is usually dark, mysterious, brooding, and living an immoral life in a vain attempt to escape unhappy memories. Heathcliff exhibits all of these characteristics. Like all romantic heroes, he is in rebellion against society and even against the laws of the universe. Byron himself had a scandalous affair with his half sister, defying the laws of church and state, and his various romantic and political exploits were the talk of all Europe. Like the Byronic hero, Rochester leads a lonely wandering life and is iconoclastic in disavowing the validity of his marriage to Bertha. He feels no guilt about his immoral life with a series of mistresses, since he does not consider himself married, but he does feel disgust at the depths of his efforts to escape his past. The Romantics believed that only negative social conditioning made people believe that Satan, Cain, and Napoleon (or even incest, atheism, and revolution) were evil. While Charlotte was too Christian and too conservative to admire Satan or Cain, she does want us to sympathize with Rochester. Emily is more unrestrained in her characterization of Heathcliff, who would gladly, like Rochester, be a bigamist, but who will stop at nothing to achieve his aim and to have his revenge.

Another characteristic of Romantic literature is the description of childhood thoughts and experiences as unique and precious. Childhood, for the Romantics, came to be seen as the time when we see things as they really are, before education, prejudice, and habit blind us to the truth. Poets like Blake and Wordsworth wrote that unless we revere the "inner child" and hold on to him, we will lose our freedom and our power. Although the narrator in *Jane Eyre* is really Jane Rochester, married ten years, the book often reads as if it is narrated by the child or adolescent Jane. This use of the first person to represent a child's point of view was new in fiction, because Charlotte Brontë was possibly the first novelist to hold that a child's point of view can be more accurate and acute than an adult's. Emily's *Wuthering Heights* is a lament on lost childhood freedom and intensity, when the spirit is less restrained by social laws and customs, and even by the body itself. The entire plot is motivated by childhood memories that Heathcliff and Catherine cannot forget, because only then were they really living. Both Charlotte and Emily never doubted that the child, as Wordsworth said, can "see into the life of things."

Romantic literature aims to change the reader's beliefs not through the intellect but through the emotions, to arouse in the reader passions and sympathies that he didn't have before. Both Charlotte and Emily make use of romantic psychology when they describe the minds and thoughts of characters during intense moments and states of excitement, when the usually insignificant can become very significant. The Brontës also make use of symbolic dreams in their novels, demonstrating the Romantic fascination with dreams and visions. The Romantics were the first to recognize the symbolic significance of dreams and to speculate on how dreams can influence our waking lives.

Both Charlotte and Emily present characters who experience intense relationships with nature, which was also a romantic preoccupation. The Romantics believed that the relationship between mind and nature is a mystical one, because there is a transcendent or divine element within nature that finds a living response within the heart of every person who is open to receive it. Jane Eyre's mind is opened to nature's healing and guiding influence several times—among them, when Nature tells her to "Flee temptation" and when Nature delivers to her the voice of Rochester calling her name. The title character in *Shirley* communes with Mother Nature rather than with a patriarchal God, and, in *Wuthering Heights*, both Heathcliff and Catherine seem to belong more to the natural than the human world. There is a constant tension in these novels between traditional patriarchal Christianity and a more Romantic animism, a belief that Nature itself is a part of God, filled with and expressing His spirit.

THE NOVEL AS A GENRE

The novel was a new form of prose fiction created in the eighteenth century by writers such as Daniel Defoe and Samuel Richardson. As opposed to the romance, which dealt with knights and ladies in highly allegorical settings, the novel dealt with ordinary people who are individuals rather than types, realistic settings, and everyday events. The novel was the literary form preferred by the bourgeoisie, because it dealt with individuals trying to make their way in a world where social mobility had become possible, though still unlikely. When Rochester, a landed gentleman, proposes to Jane Eyre, a governess, the middle-class preoccupation with upward mobility is represented as it never would have been before the rise of the novel. Such unlikely matches and elevations of social status were also the subjects of what are widely considered the first two novels ever written—Daniel Defoe's *Moll Flanders* (1722) and Samuel Richardson's *Pamela* (1740).

Eighteenth-century novels tended to emphasize incident and plot. Sir Walter Scott, the most popular early nineteenth-century novelist and one whom Charlotte greatly admired, still emphasized plot over character development in his historical novels. The historical novel, a genre invented by Scott, recreates a past historical age, including real people and real events, but introduces into this history fictitious characters, whose passions and adventures we are allowed to witness. Scott's *Waverly* (1814) follows the adventures of Waverly, a fictional character, as he enlists in the British army in 1745, then defects to the side of the Pretender Prince Charles Edward, a real historical figure whom Waverly meets in person. *Ivanhoe* (1819) is about a fictional Saxon knight of the Middle Ages who accompanies the historical King Richard the Lion-Hearted to the Crusades and returns to battle with the Norman conquerors. The novels make historical events more immediate by allowing us to experience them through characters we can know so well only because they are fictional. However, the fictional characters are not more important than the historical events.

The style developed by Jane Austen, the other most popular novelist of the Romantic period, is known as the novel of manners. The plots of these novels emphasize the behavior of characters in social settings rather than their inner conflicts. In *Pride and Prejudice* (1813), the main character, Elizabeth Bennet, must learn how to negotiate the complex social world of the landed gentry and their acquaintances. Her matrimonial future depends upon interpreting slight nuances of behavior correctly and on not making any mistakes in conduct herself, since characters in the novel of manners almost never meet privately, outside social situations, unless they are engaged or ruined. The high point of a Jane Austen novel can be a glance between two people across a crowded room. Passion and true confessions are not allowable in such a world. One must play by the social rules of the game. Charlotte was not an admirer of Jane Austen, whom she considered too emotionally distant from her characters, too lacking in passion, intensity, and poetry.

The novel of manners usually satirizes the mistakes characters make in conducting themselves and in interpreting the conduct of others. Often society itself is satirized for valuing the wrong types of conduct and the wrong types of people. The rules of the game often allow the wicked to deceive the innocent and the crassly materialistic to succeed while the sincerely romantic wilt by the wayside.

Domestic fiction, another popular genre, described middle-class family life in realistic detail, with the aim of instilling moral values in the reader. One of the best-known examples is William Goldsmith's *The Vicar of Wakefield* (1766), which describes the family life of a good clergyman. Neither the novel of manners nor the domestic novel could serve as vehicles for the intense, abnormal, and far from moral domestic situations the Brontës describe.

Both Charlotte and Emily refused to imitate any previous novelists, and they purposefully set out on their own to develop something new. Charlotte wrote to her publisher in September 1848, "Were I obliged to copy any former novelist, even the greatest, even Scott, in anything, I would not write—Unless I have something of my own to say, and a way of my own to say it in, I have no business to publish." The critic Irene Tayler claims that before the Brontës, poetry was valued as the highest form of literature, the most capable of expressing eternal truths and spiritual, transcendental experiences. The novel was about experiences in the world, not inner feelings. But the Brontës altered this view of the novel by showing that the genre could express the interior world of feelings as well as or better than poetry, thus helping the novel to become a highly respected literary genre.

Before the Brontës, novels had a dubious reputation for several reasons. First, they were not considered to be "literary" in the way that poetry was literary. They were not full of classical allusions, and their authors did not have to demonstrate, within their works, a knowledge and mastery of the entire literary tradition beginning with the Greeks. Second, novels often depicted unseemly characters of low status, involved in indecorous activities. Moll Flanders is a thief and a prostitute; Tom Jones is a fornicator, and Pamela is a servant hotly pursued by her employer. Novels were therefore considered immoral and dangerous, more likely to inflame lust and encourage illicit activity than to improve morals and manners. The Gothic novel developed at the end of the eighteenth century sought to arouse intense emotions through mystery, suspense, and sexual innuendo heightened by the supernatural, and this emphasis on melodrama was seen as low class, immoral, and unliterary. Horace Walpole's *The Castle of Otranto* (1765) is often considered the first novel in this genre, while *The Monk* (1796) by Matthew "Monk" Lewis was famous for its immorality. Mary Shelley's *Frankenstein* (1818) is perhaps the best-known example of a gothic novel with a serious purpose. Characterized by haunted castles, ghosts, immoral villains, damsels in distress, monsters, dungeons, terror, madness, and irrational events, the gothic novel was extremely popular but not quite respectable.

Charlotte and Emily Brontë both make use of gothic elements, and both seek to arouse intense emotions. Both *Jane Eyre* and *Villette* were criticized for concerning themselves so much with the desires and passions of governesses and schoolteachers, as if this were in poor taste, an unseemly blending of the Gothic with the prosaic. *Wuthering Heights* was widely considered to be extremely violent and immoral, depicting the lowest forms of human behavior and illicit passion. However, the novels' great power, consummate artistry, and seriousness of purpose allowed few to doubt their literary merit. While *Wuthering Heights* was so unique that its greatness could not be fully appreciated until the twentieth century, *Jane Eyre* was both a best-seller and a highly lauded literary achievement.

Although the Brontës did not want to imitate any other novelists, their work was of course influenced by previous writers and genres. *Jane Eyre*, for example, is a highly literary novel influenced by several different genres. It has the form of a bildungsroman, or novel of education or development, because it follows the maturation of the central character from childhood to young adulthood as she learns about the world and how to live in it. In fact, it is considered the first female bildungsroman, since that form, initiated by Goethe in *Wilhem Meister's Lehrjahre* (1795) was always about a male central character. Female "education" was almost an oxymoron until the end of the nineteenth century, and the inner life of a female child was uncharted until Charlotte Brontë's groundbreaking work.

Jane Eyre also has the structure of a spiritual autobiography or spiritual quest novel, in which the hero must overcome many pitfalls until finally finding God and salvation. St. Augustine's *Confessions* (397–398) began the tradition of the spiritual autobiography, and John Bunyan's *Pilgrim's Progress* (1678) was the most influential fictional example of this form throughout the eighteenth and nineteenth centuries.

The Brontë novels also combine elements of the romance with elements of a realistic novel. A "realistic" novel is one that deals with the everyday domestic affairs of ordinary people, does not stray from the ordinary world of cause and effect into the supernatural world, and does not overemphasize its symbolism or coincidences to the point of allegory. A romance, on the other hand, concerns characters who are extraordinary, such as kings, queens, gods, and goddesses, who are barely if at all restrained by worldly circumstances from expressing their great passions and pursuing their lofty desires, who may be aided or hindered by supernatural beings, and who live in a world not littered with everyday paraphernalia such as governesses, cows, and dead rabbits. *Jane*

Eyre is realistic in depicting the life of a lowly governess who is not transformed into a queen but remains "plain Jane" throughout the novel and whose exploits would not have been considered worthy of comment before the mid-eighteenth century. Most of the plot stays within the everyday world of cause and effect. Even the supernatural voice calling Jane to "resist temptation" and then calling her back to Rochester can be seen as an externalization of her own conscience and her own desires. But many references and comparisons to fairies, ghosts, vampires, haunted castles, ghouls, and other supernatural beings and places lend the novel a gothic air. The overly symbolic nature of names and appearances lend it the air of allegory, and the highly unlikely coincidences, such as Jane's being rescued from starvation by her own unknown cousins and her receiving a large inheritance from an unknown uncle, are more reminiscent of fairy tale or romance than realism. *Wuthering Heights* is an even more unusual mix of the romantic and the realistic. No one had dared to describe the familial abuse and violence not uncommon within many isolated cottages and farmhouses with more realistic detail than had Emily. Novels were, after all, marketed to middle class readers who were or aspired to be genteel. Even when the author was thought to be a man, many readers were outraged by the coarse language and savagery. But despite its grimly realistic domestic brutality, it would be hard to find a hero in a nineteenth-century realistic novel more unrestrained in his passions than Heathcliff, a more romantic heroine than Catherine, or a more haunting sense of the supernatural than that which permeates the novel.

RECURRING THEMES

Both Charlotte and Emily Brontë depict women struggling against restrictions imposed on them by a patriarchal if not feudalistic society. The feeling or the actual situation of being imprisoned recurs in many of the novels. In *Wuthering Heights*, the elder Catherine feels imprisoned by her brother and by Joseph the servant, and she escapes by running away to the moors with Heathcliff. Later she will feel imprisoned to the point of longing for death at her husband Edgar Linton's home, begging only that the window be opened so that she can smell the air of freedom before she dies. Her daughter Cathy grows up at the Linton estate isolated from the world, enclosed by a stone wall, like Sleeping Beauty waiting for release. When she finally releases herself, jumping the wall of the Grange with her pony and escaping to Wuthering Heights, she soon finds herself imprisoned by a much more terrible ogre than Mrs. Dean. Heathcliff cruelly and violently imprisons her at Wuthering Heights until she marries Linton, and even after her marriage, he will not allow her to leave to see her dying father.

Jane Eyre is imprisoned in the Red Room by her aunt, a terrifying experience that symbolizes all the forces acting against Jane's self-development. Lowood school is run like a prison, and after escaping that servitude, Jane finds herself employed at a home where her employer's wife has been secretly imprisoned in the attic for years. Jane's entire story can be read as an escape from various imprisoning situations or roles, such as rich man's mistress or missionary's pseudo-wife. Like Jane Eyre, Caroline Helstone in Charlotte's next novel, *Shirley*, is imprisoned by her position as a single woman without a fortune. She is literally dying for lack of love and occupation, because she has no outlet through which to express herself and develop her potential. Lucy Snowe, in *Villette*, feels imprisoned and buried alive in the boarding school where she works and where she almost loses her mind. A nun was supposedly buried alive in the garden of the school when it was a convent, symbolizing the fate of all women who transgress the restrictions imposed on them by traditional society.

All of the Brontë heroines are orphans, and the theme of homelessness also recurs through Charlotte's novels. Charlotte and Emily lost their mother when they were very young, and the death of their eldest sister Maria, who had acted as a mother figure after their mother's death, must have affected both Charlotte and Emily deeply. The homelessness affecting Charlotte's heroines requires further examination, however, since Charlotte spent most of her life in her father's home. Jane Eyre and Lucy Snowe have no parents and no home, highlighting their starkly existential position in the world. There is no role they can easily assume, such as daughter, sister, wife—no automatic acceptance anywhere, no security, no ready-made identity. They must create themselves from nothing, because they have neither money nor family. Caroline Helstone, whose father is dead and whose mother has abandoned her, feels the same kind of existential unhappiness since her uncle, a misogynist, completely ignores her. The feeling of not being at home in the world, which haunts all of Charlotte's heroines, may reflect her uneasiness in the society of any but her family, since everyone seemed to misjudge her mind and talents because of her tiny body, plain face, and shy demeanor. As daughters of a poor clergyman, both she and Emily were square pegs that wouldn't quite fit through the round holes carved out for them by society. Charlotte experienced loneliness and an isolating sense of strangeness as a foreigner and a Protestant in Catholic Belgium and seldom left home again after returning to England, although she was less loath to leave home than was Emily. Charlotte was received into London society as a famous novelist, but here she was even more of a misfit than in Belgium, and the glittering literati only laughed at her behind her back.

The theme of homelessness is handled quite differently in *Wuthering Heights*, where characters are passionately attached to their first home and feel wretched despair when separated from it, as if their very identity resided in the parental home and had to be left behind with it. Catherine, Cathy, and Isabella Linton experience this despair, and Hindley may well have experienced it when he was sent to school, since he returns no better for the experience but determined to exact revenge on the foster son who had stolen his place in his father's heart. Even Heathcliff cannot leave behind his foster home, returning after three years as if irresistibly drawn back to find the other half of his soul. The world of Wuthering Heights is strangely narrow: there doesn't seem to be any place other than "home." Where Heathcliff came from, or where he was during his three-year sojourn, is never described, and Isabella's residence in London is similarly left a blank. Even the village of Gimmerton, which lies below the Grange and Wuthering Heights, is left strangely without concrete features, as if once one left the small area that surrounds the two houses of Wuthering Heights and Thrushcross Grange, one falls off the face of the earth. Perhaps Emily, when away from home, felt as if she had landed on another planet with a strange atmosphere she could not breathe, surrounded by creatures that couldn't speak her language. Charlotte wrote that Emily always sickened when away from the parsonage and rarely spoke to anyone, even when directly addressed. Biographers agree that Emily's world was narrow but deep, intensely imaginative and spiritual rather than social.

LITERARY INFLUENCE

The best-known eighteenth-century novelists were men, and their fictions were usually about male protagonists. The only well-known female novelists before the Brontës were Jane Austen and Mary Shelley, and feminist literary critics Sandra Gilbert and Susan Gubar emphasize the Brontës' role as the most important female authors of their century. The Brontës published their novels using sexually ambiguous pseudonyms because they wanted to be judged as writers, not as female writers. They realized that novels by women would not be expected to have literary merit but would be expected to conform more strictly to Victorian standards of morality and decency. Other female authors resorted to masculine pseudonyms as well. Mary Ann Evans, a great admirer of Charlotte Brontë and often considered the greatest novelist of the nineteenth century, published under the pen name George Eliot.

The Brontës not only brought the representation of intense mental suffering and unusual states of consciousness to the novel, they also depicted the way a human mind "half perceives and half creates" experience, as William Wordsworth stated in his famous preface to the 1800 edition of *Lyrical Ballads*. The Brontës brought the metaphysics of Romanticism—the belief that human experience transcends the reasonable and logical—to the novel. The Romantics believed that imagination was more important than reason in shaping experience and that individual private experience was more important than how the individual fit into the social scheme of things. The Romantics, beginning with Rousseau, also initiated the representation of formerly private thoughts and desires, a characteristic the Brontës admired and imitated. While the Brontës were influenced by the entire canon of English literature, but especially by the Romantic poets, they in turn influenced future generations of writers. The intense interiority of Charlotte Brontë's prose greatly influenced the modernist style of Virginia Woolf, D. H. Lawrence, and William Faulkner. Her depiction of women in intense conflict with their social position and gender role has been one of the most recurring themes in women's literature throughout the twentieth century.

While Charlotte's themes and emotional intensity influenced the modernists and beyond, the structure of her novels is more conventional than that of *Wuthering Heights*. The form of Emily's novel has been highly influential. At times it seems as intricate as that of the most postmodern parodies of traditional fictional form. The story of Catherine and Heathcliff is repeated in the story of Cathy and Hareton. Different characters have the same names. Catherine Earnshaw loves Heathcliff, but she marries and becomes Catherine Linton. Catherine (Cathy) Linton loves (Linton) Heathcliff, marries and becomes Catherine Heathcliff, but then marries again and becomes Catherine Earnshaw, taking us back to the beginning, as if this story could be retold ad infinitum. *Wuthering Heights* rejects not only the conventional structure of fiction but also the conventional structure of the reality fiction is based on. Fiction, and life, is usually comprised of a series of social and familial relationships, but in *Wuthering Heights*, according to Marxist literary critic Raymond Williams, "at a peak of intensity, the complicated barriers of a system of relationships are broken through, finally, by an absolute human commitment. The commitment is realized through death, and the essential tragedy, embodied elsewhere in individual figures who may, by magic be rescued from it, becomes the form of the whole work" (69). Whereas in novels such as *Jane Eyre*, a character may magically escape from the usual bonds of class, sex, family relations, and societal limitations to marry her wealthy employer, Emily Brontë refuses to leave the social system intact at all—her characters transcend it rather than sneak around its restrictions. Catherine and Heathcliff are seen walking the moors after their deaths, having escaped from culture into nature, from the law of the land into the law of the spirit.

The novels of Charlotte and Emily Brontë continue to be widely read and highly influential. Many new critical studies of their works are published every year, and new biographies continue to be written as well. Movie versions of the novels continue to be produced, and many web sites are devoted to their life and works. Twentieth-century authors take these timeless works and revise them into new forms. Jean Rhys' *Wide Sargasso Sea* (1966) tells the story of *Jane Eyre* from Bertha Mason's point of view, while Jamaica Kincaid's *Annie John* (1985) examines the themes of *Jane Eyre* from a third-world Caribbean perspective. The Brontës are major contributors to our literary heritage, and their works, especially *Jane Eyre* and *Wuthering Heights*, have become part of our cultural vocabulary.

Wuthering Heights
(1847)

Emily Brontë's *Wuthering Heights* is one of the most enigmatic classics in English literature. It seems to demand explanation and interpretation, yet totally contradictory explanations can seem equally plausible. Some critics have questioned if *Wuthering Heights* really is a novel. Perhaps it is a long prose poem, or a philosophical allegory on nature versus culture, creative talent versus culture, or the feminine versus the patriarchal. It combines elements of the realistic novel, the gothic horror story, the domestic novel, and the love story or romance, with mysticism and the supernatural thrown in for good measure. While a hidden meaning may never be pinned down, the raw power of the text has fascinated and amazed many generations of readers, while just as many generations of critics have been attracted by its complex structure and highly symbolic style.

PLOT DEVELOPMENT

Reading *Wuthering Heights* is like peeling off the layers of an onion, only to find that once all the layers are gone, there is no satisfying solution or "core" to the story. The structure, which has been described as circular, or as a series of boxes within boxes, is complex, intricately worked out, and significant. The outermost story concerns Mr. Lockwood's firsthand experiences at Wuthering Heights. The second layer concerns the story of the second Catherine, born Catherine Linton, briefly married to Linton Heathcliff, who by the end of the novel is engaged to marry Hareton Earnshaw. A yet deeper layer concerns the married life of Catherine Linton née Earnshaw, her tormented death after Heathcliff's return, Heathcliff's marriage to Isabella Linton, and his destruction of Hindley Earnshaw. Deeper still is the story of Hindley Earnshaw's despotic rule over Wuthering Heights after his father's death, and his disintegration after his wife's death. The deepest layer of the onion is the story of Heathcliff's arrival at Wuthering Heights as a child, and the relationship he and Catherine Earnshaw enjoyed. Each layer takes us further into the past. Dorothy Van Ghent and other critics describe the world of the boy Heathcliff and Catherine Earnshaw as the mythic past, the past of fairy tales, while the story of her daughter Catherine takes us into the recognizable social and historical past.

The narrator who relates the story to us is Mr. Lockwood, a foppish, bookish young gentleman driven from society by his cowardly inability to continue a mild flirtation with a young girl. Looking for solitude, he rents Thrushcross Grange, an isolated manor house in the north of England. His landlord, Mr. Heathcliff, lives a few miles up the hill at a farm called Wuthering Heights. At first Lockwood thinks that since Mr. Heathcliff is a misanthrope and a recluse, they must have a lot in common, but Mr. Lockwood, who represents the civilized world of seaside resort towns and London society, soon finds out that Mr. Heathcliff, and everyone at the Heights, lives in such degraded hatred, violence, and passion as is seldom seen in the city.

Lockwood cannot fathom the relationship between Mr. Heathcliff, Catherine Heathcliff, and Hareton Earnshaw, the three residents of the Heights (other than the two servants, Joseph and Zillah). The year is 1801, and Heathcliff is living with his daughter-in-law Catherine Heathcliff and her cousin Hareton Earnshaw. Lockwood ends up spending the night, much to Heathcliff's chagrin, because a snowstorm has obscured the way back to Thrushcross Grange. Without Heathcliff's knowledge, Zillah puts him in the only empty bedroom, where Lockwood suffers a series of terrible nightmares important to the plot.

Before falling asleep, Lockwood notices that his old-fashioned, enclosed bed is scratched over with a name variously written: Catherine Earnshaw, Catherine Heathcliff, and Catherine Linton. Next he notices a Bible, inscribed with the name Catherine Earnshaw, the margins of which have been used as a diary. The diary, written twenty-five years earlier, describes how Catherine Earnshaw and Heathcliff plan to rebel against their cruel master, Catherine's older brother Hindley, and how Hindley has banished Heathcliff from family life.

Lockwood has several nightmares. During the second nightmare, he hears a tap on the windowpane, opens it and is grabbed by the small, cold hand of a ghost-child, who begs him to let her in. When she won't let go he rubs her wrist on the broken glass till blood covers the sheets, but still she won't let go. She says she is Catherine Linton, and that she has come home after losing her way on the moor. "I've been a waif for twenty years!" she cries. Lockwood yells in his sleep, and Heathcliff comes in, hears Lockwood's dream, and rushes to the window to let in the spirit, but despite his anguished pleadings she will not return. While Lockwood never doubts that he has experienced a nightmare, Heathcliff obviously believes that the spirit is real.

Lockwood returns to Thrushcross Grange the next day and asks his housekeeper, Mrs. Nelly Dean, to explain what is going on at Wuthering Heights. Nelly Dean becomes the second narrator, who tells much of the story to Lockwood. The story of the first Catherine Earnshaw and Heathcliff is thus told to us third and sometimes fourth hand. Nelly Dean is levelheaded and unromantic, not the type to exaggerate or invent, or even to understand, the strange goings-on she has witnessed.

The story Nelly relates first is the core story, and some critics have claimed that this story explains how "civilization" was born. Nelly describes how Hindley's father, Mr. Earnshaw, brought home a dirty, starving, homeless dark-skinned child he'd found in the slums of Liverpool, and named him Heathcliff, after a son who had died young. The first Heathcliff may have been the oldest son, and this replacement Heathcliff takes his place in the father's affections, slighting the legitimate heir Hindley. Both Hindley and Catherine are outraged by the arrival of this orphan, since Hindley's present, a fiddle, has been broken, and Catherine's present, a whip, has been lost. Hindley hates Heathcliff because Mr. Earnshaw treats him as a favorite, but Catherine soon forms a close bond with him and gains a power over Heathcliff that even Mr. Earnshaw resents. Gilbert and Gubar speculate that Heathcliff becomes the "whip" Catherine wanted and needed in order to have any power or freedom as a female child.

Heathcliff bears Hindley's abuse but manages to get his own way oftener than not, because old Earnshaw loves him. Eventually Hindley is sent to school, but at old Earnshaw's death, Hindley returns, with a wife, to rule Wuthering Heights with the cruel tyranny of a weak man, determined to revenge himself on Heathcliff by turning him into a servant and farm laborer. Catherine and Heathcliff remain inseparable, however, until Catherine's introduction into the more civilized world of the Lintons.

Heathcliff and Catherine have run away from home and have been scampering across the moors. Heathcliff beats her at a race because she has lost her shoes in the bog. They observe the wealthy Linton household through the window, but the Linton bulldog attacks the intruders, biting Catherine's foot. This bite is often interpreted as the twelve-year-old Catherine's sexual initiation, because she is taken into the Linton household and made into a fine lady.

Heathcliff stays to rescue Catherine from this prison, but looking through the window he is surprised to find that she is being made much of and enjoying it immensely. Perhaps Cathy's losing her shoes represents the handicap of her approaching sexual maturity, with the concomitant loss of her prepubescent equality and freedom. Doomed to lose the race with Heathcliff, she must choose between nature and culture, brute force or legalistic, capitalistic power.

Catherine's return from Thrushcross Grange five weeks later creates a great conflict in her heart. She likes to be the center of attention and to be dressed in fine clothes, but she is miserable because Heathcliff has been violently excluded from her new world. For a time she attempts to live in both worlds, acting like a lady with Edgar Linton and like her old self with Heathcliff, trying to make sure the two never meet. But Heathcliff knows he is being slighted, and she finally tells him his company is not pleasurable, because he knows nothing, says nothing, and cannot "amuse" her. She and Heathcliff have lived in a prelinguistic state of unity, but Catherine is fascinated by the more social world, where she can be admired as an individual. She becomes proud and ambitious, the queen of the neighborhood, although we never see her meet anyone except the Lintons.

By entering the world of language, Catherine is entering the laws of the patriarchy, and leaving behind a preverbal level of connection to another human being and to her own soul and heart. She thinks she will be able to control Edgar Linton and use him as a tool to help Heathcliff, but Heathcliff runs away before he can even hear that this is her plan. On the same day she accepts Edgar's marriage proposal, Catherine becomes so distraught at losing Heathcliff that she becomes violently ill. Ironically, her illness kills Edgar Linton's parents, who take her in during her recuperation, thus clearing the way for her to be the finest lady in the neighborhood.

Catherine seems to forget about Heathcliff after she returns from the Grange for the second time, and within three years has married Edgar Linton, because he is rich and kind and docile. She seems to be happily married, but when Heathcliff unexpectedly returns about five months after her marriage, she is overjoyed, and suddenly cannot live without him again. Her entire courtship and marriage to Edgar Linton have been but "a sleep and a forgetting," and she suddenly awakens to a full realization of what she has lost. Catherine hopes to again have both Heathcliff and Edgar in her life, sure that Edgar loves her too much to cross her in anything, and that Heathcliff loves her too much to injure anyone she cares for. She is soon proven wrong. Heathcliff tells her that he is her slave, but others are his slaves to torture as she tortures him. Nelly notes that "the spirit which served her was growing intractable: she could neither lay nor control it" (88). Heathcliff warns Catherine that he will marry Isabella to revenge himself on Edgar and will not be appeased by mere words:

"Having levelled my palace, don't erect a hovel and complacently admire your own charity in giving me that for a home" (87). Catherine is Heathcliff's palace, but without Heathcliff the palace is empty, and both suffer a gaping wound in their souls.

Edgar demands that Catherine choose either himself or Heathcliff, but she would rather die than make this choice, and retreats to her room to starve herself to death, in order to break their hearts. While Catherine lies dangerously ill, she deliriously imagines that she is a child again, then desperately wishes to be in her old bed at her old house. But her old bed, the one that Lockwood slept in, is very similar to a coffin, and Catherine knows that she cannot return there except by dying. She relives the despair of being separated from Heathcliff after her father's death, and cannot remember what had caused her to reject Heathcliff in the first place. She feels as if she had been violently wrenched from her home when she was twelve, "and been converted at a stroke into Mrs. Linton, the lady of Thrushcross Grange, and the wife of a stranger; an exile, and outcast, thenceforth, from what had been my world" (97). She longs to be a girl again, "half savage, and hardy, and free" (97), instead of a woman, a prisoner at Thrushcross Grange, forced into the unnatural role of wife and mother. Catherine is pregnant but never mentions this; rather than become a mother to a Linton, she would much rather return to childhood herself, or die. She imagines daring Heathcliff to accompany her and says if he does, "I'll not lie there by myself, they may bury me twelve feet deep, and throw the church down over me, but I won't rest till you are with me. I never will" (98). Her desire to die, and to thus be reunited with an essential part of herself, reinforces the theory that Heathcliff symbolizes some primal component of her spirit.

Catherine lies ill for two months. Meanwhile, Heathcliff has eloped with Isabella to revenge himself on Edgar Linton. The Lintons seem fatally attracted to the violence of the Heights. Just as Edgar had proposed to Catherine after she had hit him, Isabella runs away with Heathcliff even though she has just seen him hang her dog. Heathcliff plans to get back at Edgar by torturing his sister, always keeping within the limits of the law to make sure that his prey cannot legally escape. His plan seems to be to drive Edgar Linton into some kind of furious duel and so to finish him off. Heathcliff and Isabella return after two months, to live at Wuthering Heights, and Heathcliff immediately demands to see Catherine, even though Nelly warns him that he is endangering her life if he does.

The final meeting between Heathcliff and Catherine is passionate, violent, cruel, and heartbreaking. "I wish I could hold you till we were both dead!" Catherine cries, and seems to resent the fact that Heathcliff won't immediately commit suicide (123). She longs only to escape the prison of her body "into that glorious world, and to be always there; not seeing it dimly through tears, and yearning for it through the walls of an aching heart; but really with it, and in it" (124). Heathcliff, however, blames Catherine for betraying her own heart by leaving him, thus killing herself, and him. "You, of your own will did it," he claims, and mourns that after her death his soul will be in the grave (125). Catherine reminds Heathcliff that he left her also, and Heathcliff says that he can forgive his murderer, Catherine, but cannot forgive her murderer, himself.

Catherine dies that night, after delivering a premature infant who will be named Cathy. Catherine's death occurs halfway through the novel, or at the center of the circular plot. Heathcliff now concentrates his energies on revenging himself on all his enemies, using their weapons—land, money, marriage, and inheritance. He finally allows Isabella to escape his guardianship, and she settles elsewhere and has his child, Linton Heathcliff. Hindley drinks himself to death, having mortgaged all his land to Heathcliff, who now becomes sole owner of Wuthering Heights. Heathcliff raises Hindley's son Hareton, who would have been the heir, to be a servant and an illiterate brute in order to revenge himself on Hindley by degrading his son. Although Hareton is not Heathcliff's ward, Heathcliff threatens to send for his own son if the Lintons attempt to take Hareton from him.

Having gained possession of Wuthering Heights and Hindley's son, Heathcliff next moves to gain possession of Thrushcross Grange and Cathy Linton. After Isabella's death, Heathcliff demands custody of his son Linton because Linton is heir to Thrushcross Grange. Seeing how weak and sickly Linton is, Heathcliff decides that his son must marry Cathy, to make sure that Thrushcross Grange does not revert to her after Linton's death, and also to secure the personal property of the Grange, which would certainly go to Cathy upon her father's death. Heathcliff wants to degrade and trample upon everything belonging to the Lintons and the Earnshaws, and this includes his own son Linton and his beloved's daughter Cathy.

Cathy has been raised in complete ignorance of having a cousin named Hareton, and has never been anywhere except to chapel. Until she is thirteen years old, Cathy doesn't even know that Wuthering Heights exists. While her father is away at his dying sister's house, Cathy escapes Nelly's watchful eye and rambles up the hill looking for Penistone Crags. She first meets Hareton, then eighteen years old, when her dogs get into a fight with his dogs. She and Hareton have an interesting time together but quarrel when she, confused about his social position, begins to treat him like a servant. Cathy is appalled to learn that Hareton is her cousin, and later treats Hareton with even more scorn and contempt when encouraged by her other cousin, Linton Heathcliff.

Isabella had hoped her brother would raise her son Linton after her death, but Heathcliff immediately demands the child as his "property," planning to force Linton into giving up Thrushcross Grange after Edgar's death or making his father his heir. However, Linton's poor health threatens to foil Heathcliff's plan, for if Linton Heathcliff dies before Edgar Linton, then Thrushcross Grange would probably become Cathy's property, as she would be the next surviving heir. Heathcliff tells Nelly that the entail on Wuthering Heights (discussed below) does not specifically guarantee Cathy the inheritance, but neither would Heathcliff clearly be the successor. Therefore, to avoid a legal battle, and to ensure that all of the movable property at Thrushcross Grange also becomes his, Heathcliff forces his dying son Linton to play the suitor to Cathy.

Cathy and Linton like each other, and Nelly hasn't the power to keep them apart. Edgar Linton, Cathy's father, does not object to the possible marriage because he thinks this is the only way Cathy could continue to live at Thrushcross Grange, but he refuses to allow Cathy to visit Wuthering Heights. Cathy and Linton secretly carry on a correspondence, with Heathcliff editing Linton's letters. When Nelly puts a stop to the correspondence, Heathcliff catches Cathy accidentally locked outside the walls of the Grange, and reprimands her for breaking Linton's heart. Cathy insists on visiting Linton, and their relationship wavers comically between childish love and childish hatred. After that first visit, Nelly catches a terrible cold, and while both she and Edgar are ill, Cathy secretly continues her visits to the Heights.

Her visits are discovered and cut off, and Heathcliff does not allow Linton to visit the Grange, to prevent Edgar from seeing how sick he is. Instead, Heathcliff makes Linton write letters asking to meet Cathy halfway between the Heights and Thrushcross Grange. Finally Edgar agrees. Nelly and Cathy set off to meet Linton, and find him lying on the heath, much closer to his own house than the Grange, so ill he can scarcely walk and so frightened by his father's threats that he insists he is better. They agree to meet a week later. Cathy's father is clearly dying, but Nelly thinks it will do her good to get out of the sickroom, so she insists that Cathy keep her promise. They find Linton even more terrified than before. He claims he will be killed if Catherine leaves him. When Heathcliff joins their party, Linton almost faints with terror and will not let go of Cathy's arm. Cathy feels his desperation and can't help breaking her father's command not to enter the Heights, but as soon as she and Nelly enter, Heathcliff locks them in and says neither shall leave until Cathy marries Linton.

Desperate to see her dying father, Cathy agrees, and evidently they are married during the four days Nelly is locked away in a different room. The minister must be Heathcliff's paid servant as much as the lawyer will prove to be, since the entire countryside think that Nelly and Cathy have been drowned in the bog. But when Nelly is finally released, she finds that Cathy is still a prisoner, and Linton is exulting over his new property rights as owner of everything Cathy formerly possessed, including the locket she wears around her neck with pictures of her mother and father. Finally Linton helps Cathy escape, in time to see her father before he dies. Edgar had planned to change his will so that the movable property at Thrushcross Grange would be protected by trustees, but the lawyer, who has sold himself to Heathcliff, delays arriving until Edgar is dead, and Heathcliff strolls in the next day to take over his domain, firing all the servants except Nelly.

While Edward is being buried next to Catherine, Heathcliff bribes the sexton to let him loosen one side of her coffin, and of his as well when he is buried beside her, so that their dust can mingle and "by the time Linton gets to us, he'll not know which is which!" (218). Heathcliff's enemies are now all dead, and he realizes that the only way he can truly revenge himself on them is if their spirits return to earth, or at the resurrection.

Heathcliff forces Cathy to return to Wuthering Heights and live with Linton, but Linton dies just a few days after she returns. His father refuses to send for a doctor, saying "his life is not worth a farthing, and I won't spend a farthing on him" (221). Heathcliff has forced Linton to write a will making his father heir to all his and his wife's movable property, leaving Cathy destitute and in his power. Although Heathcliff is not heir to Thrushcross Grange, since his son, being a minor, could not will his estate to another, he is nevertheless in possession of them and Cathy doesn't have the money or the power to dispute his possession. This is how Lockwood finds Cathy at the beginning of his narrative—sullen, bitter, and hateful to everyone, especially Hareton.

Lockwood leaves Thrushcross Grange in January, after he recovers from his illness, even though he is obligated to continue renting it for a year. Finding himself in the neighborhood in September, however, he decides to spend the night there, but finds that Nelly Dean has moved back to Wuthering Heights. Lockwood learns that Heathcliff is dead. Nelly describes how Heathcliff lost interest in all things earthly, including the growing friendship between Cathy and Hareton. He seemed to see the dead Catherine before him, and became unable to eat or sleep. He felt close to attaining his heaven—reunion with Catherine in death—and one morning Nelly finds him lying in the old cabinet-bed that he and Catherine once shared, dead, with "a frightful, life-like gaze of exultation" in his eyes (254). The window is open and the bed is rain-soaked, implying that his spirit has slipped out the window, joining Catherine's on the moor.

Heathcliff is buried as he directed, next to Catherine, with her husband's coffin lying on the other side. The two panels separating Heathcliff's and Catherine's bodies are removed, so that their dust can mingle. The country folks see Heathcliff's and Catherine's ghosts walking together across the moors, although neither Nelly nor Lockwood can believe that they do not lie at peace. Cathy and Hareton are engaged to be married on New Year's Day, and plan to move to Thrushcross Grange, leaving Joseph as caretaker of Wuthering

Heights. The plot has come full circle: Cathy, as beautiful and haughty as her mother, has not disdained to marry her cousin Hareton, who has been as degraded as Heathcliff ever was. Hareton holds no grudges against anyone, least of all Heathcliff, and the two original families are joined happily at last.

CHARACTER DEVELOPMENT

Does *Wuthering Heights* even have characters? The characters are all so similar that they seem to be mere parts of persons. The repetitions in plot emphasize the "sameness" of all the characters, while famous statements like Catherine's "I am Heathcliff!" add to the impression that these characters are strangely melded into each other. Characters mistake each other and see the image of one person in another. For example, when Isabella flings her food down in a fit of passion at Wuthering Heights, Joseph says, "Weel done, Miss Cathy!" (112). Any woman having a fit of passion at Wuthering Heights because she is powerless there is designated "Miss Cathy."

The most enigmatic character, Heathcliff, has created the most disagreement. Who or what is Heathcliff? Nelly knows everything about him "except where he was born, and who were his parents, and how he got his money" (27), but these unknowns are the very foundations of identity in any society. Perhaps he is a prince in disguise, kidnapped and brought to England. Perhaps, as old Earnshaw comments, he may have come not from God but from the devil (28). Many critics believe that Heathcliff represents the daemonic, that inhuman, primal energy of nature, as well as the primal energy of the unconscious mind. Like Freud's id (discussed in the last section of Chapter 6), he knows neither morals, restraints, human laws, nor consequences for breaking them. Within the novel, words such as "devil," "vampire," and "ghoul" are used to describe him.

Heathcliff alternates between victim and persecutor. At first he is abused and rejected by the Earnshaw household, but soon he is tyrannizing over the much older Hindley, forcing him to exchange colts and daring him to tell his father. When Hindley becomes master of Wuthering Heights, he immediately turns Heathcliff into a servant and farm laborer, cruelly extinguishing any impulse Heathcliff had to be good. Heathcliff and Hindley seem locked in a struggle to the death to be the firstborn son, the man with the power, and their battle can be seen as symbolic of the unrefined struggle for male primacy, when it is not disguised by societal conventions.

Heathcliff becomes sullen, unkempt, and ignorant. He broods only upon revenge, but he doesn't leave the Heights until he overhears that Catherine won't marry him because it will degrade her. Three years later, Heathcliff returns, in appearance a wealthy gentleman. His ability to transform himself so quickly from brute to gentleman is indicative of his intelligence, determination, energy, and ruthlessness. Catherine is overjoyed at seeing him, to the chagrin of her husband. The desire between Heathcliff and Catherine is much more than sexual; according to one critic, it is a "desire for more being" (Bersani 213), a desire to fill a lack in one's self that can't be satisfied by any particular experience or pleasure. No actual relationship, including that of man and wife, can fulfill their desire and need for each other. Heathcliff and Catherine form such a close bond that many readers have felt they are not really two separate human beings. Their childhood bond was an intimacy that obliterated the boundaries of identity similar to the melding of souls with God after death, but their joy broke the laws of God and the corporal world, dooming it to destruction.

Although he had planned only to look at Catherine, then kill Hindley and himself, Heathcliff is no more able to tear himself away from Catherine than she is from him. Catherine calls him a "fierce, pitiless, wolfish man" and warns Isabella away from him, but Isabella is fascinated by his perversity. Since Heathcliff is only nineteen when he returns a rich man and begins his coldly calculated and shrewdly executed plan of revenge, his power combined with his youth suggest something otherworldly, sinister, and fiendish about him.

Heathcliff can act a better gentleman than Hindley and look to have more breeding and dignity than does Isabella. Nelly observes that "so much had circumstances altered their positions, that he would certainly have struck a stranger as a born and bred gentleman, and his wife as a thorough little slattern!" (114). His only purpose is to degrade and destroy the two houses that have rejected him. He entices Hindley into gambling away his estate and plans to drive Edgar mad by torturing his sister, thus precipitating a confrontation during which he can kill Edgar in self-defense.

Catherine's death shatters Heathcliff, as if she were just as much a part of him as he of her: "I *cannot* live without my life! I *cannot* live without my soul!" he howls like an animal. But he then systematically and cold-bloodedly continues to revenge himself on all of the Lintons and Earnshaws. Many readers no longer sympathize with Heathcliff after Catherine's death, feeling that he becomes a heartless monster, but other readers feel that his continued revenge is justified and morally appropriate, as if the Lintons and Earnshaws deserve this whipping at the hands of fate. Isabella, who soon after Catherine's death is allowed to escape from Wuthering Heights, claims that Heathcliff is "not a human being" (133). When Heathcliff becomes owner of Wuthering Heights and master to Hareton, he plans to degrade Hareton even further than he himself was degraded by Hindley. He sends for his own son Linton only to use him mercilessly as a tool for his further revenge. He forces Cathy to marry Linton just to make sure that she also is entirely destitute, since all her possessions become her husband's property. But he seems to get less and less pleasure from his revenge and waits only for death to reunite him with Catherine. Catherine had claimed that he was an avaricious man, but he acquires properties only for revenge, not because he wants them for any reason. He can't even force himself to write a will disposing of his property, wishing only that he "could annihilate it from the face of the earth" (252). Like Catherine, he seems to starve himself to death, but unintentionally, finding that he cannot eat. His face in death wears a look of exultation, as if the final, perfect, complete, and eternal union both he and Catherine had always yearned for has finally taken place.

Heathcliff's hand has been cut by the same lattice that had cut the ghostly Catherine's hand in Lockwood's dream, but Heathcliff's corporal body doesn't bleed, suggesting to some that he has been dead all along, or at least since Catherine's death. Heathcliff's desire for Catherine can be interpreted as the greatest expression of romantic love, the desire to completely merge with the beloved object. He may also represent some part of Catherine's psyche, such as her "male muse," as critic Irene Tayler claims, which Emily Brontë herself rejected by agreeing to publish her poetry—a step toward ambition and the world's values equivalent to Catherine's marrying Edgar Linton.

Heathcliff and the first Catherine, born Earnshaw, have such an intense, mysterious bond that many readers feel Catherine also represents the Freudian id, or untamed nature. She requests a whip as a present, is high spirited and mischievous, and becomes as wild as a heathen after her father's death, until that fateful day when she is taken into Thrushcross Grange after being bitten, and Heathcliff is barred entry. Catherine is always selfish and self-centered, but she is uncalculating in her selfishness and capable of winning over even those she has injured grievously. Nelly says that when she made another cry, she "would oblige you to be quiet that you might comfort her" (33), rather than that she might comfort the person she has injured. The Linton parents and even Hindley's wife conspire to make a lady out of Catherine, with the express purpose of separating her from Heathcliff, and they succeed. Becoming a lady involves a symbolic crippling of her foot, as well as the real weight of expensive dresses and riding habits. Catherine is elevated into the prison house of a role and a function—the role of middle-class wife and the function of giving birth. Therefore, when Catherine says Heathcliff is "more myself than I am," she means that her real self has been left behind, where Heathcliff lives.

Catherine accepts Edgar Linton's proposal of marriage in order to exchange a brutal tyrant, her brother, for someone she thinks she can control, the mild-mannered Edgar. Marrying Edgar is the only way she can acquire any power, and she plans to use this power to help Heathcliff escape from Hindley's violence. As soon as Heathcliff runs away, Catherine becomes violently ill with a fever, symbolizing some kind of violent rending of the spirit. Upon recovering, she is just as arrogant and ambitious as ever, marries Edgar, and seems to live as a happily married wife until Heathcliff returns. However, after Heathcliff's return, she feels life welling up in her again, and she confesses to Nelly that she has been often bitterly miserable and "in angry rebellion against providence" because of Heathcliff's disappearance (77).

Heathcliff's return leads directly to her death. Her unabashed joy at seeing him irritates her husband to tears, and when the two men quarrel Catherine again becomes violently ill, seemingly by design. She does not want to elope with Heathcliff—she wants to have both men in her life, and she interprets Edgar's jealousy as a lack of love. Catherine locks herself in her room, intending to starve herself to death, which can be interpreted as a refusal to become a woman, even though she is pregnant, or a refusal to play the role of a wife, owned by only one man. She wants to return to childhood, to Wuthering Heights, before she had to make such impossible choices. She doesn't recognize her face in the mirror, as if she doesn't recognize the woman she has become. She dreams that she becomes a child again and feels that everything that has happened to her since her father's death has never happened, that she has been violently transplanted into an alien house and an alien role. Rather than developing as a character, Catherine has come full circle, back to her beginnings as a wild child wandering the moors, at one with nature and at odds with society. She has only played the part of wife. Her inner nature has been temporarily concealed, but it has not changed.

Several critics feel that Catherine's spirit is released at her death, to wander the moors again, but that this spirit is that of a child. This would explain why the ghost Lockwood dreams about is named Catherine Linton, even though she is a child, and Catherine Earnshaw did not marry until the age of eighteen.

Unlike her mother, Catherine's daughter Cathy does develop and change. Her return to Wuthering Heights transforms herself from a Linton into an Earnshaw, in the reverse order of her mother's transformations from an Earnshaw to a Linton, but she seems to have changed inwardly as well. Cathy, as her father calls her, grows up just as isolated as her mother had but in a more civilized environment. She is headstrong like her mother but not as selfish and wild. Social class threatens to destroy her life just as it had her mother's, when she mocks and despises Hareton, preferring her sickly cousin Linton. However, her attraction to both cousins is within the normal realm of friendship and love. After Linton's death, she continues to be haughty to Hareton until she decides to make a friend of him. Eventually she wins his trust, and by the end of the novel they are engaged to be married.

While Heathcliff may have hoped that his Catherine would outlive her milk-blooded husband Edgar and return to him, Cathy is lucky enough to outlive her first marriage, based on superficial class compatibility, and to move on to a worthier love. Instead of feeling that such a marriage would degrade her, Cathy works to improve Hareton's education and manners. Even though Heathcliff thinks that he has degraded Hareton to the point where "he's safe from her love" (166), Cathy has matured enough to truly love and appreciate Hareton. Most readers feel that their union is the resolution to the conflict precipitated by Heathcliff's arrival.

Catherine's brother Hindley Earnshaw was already a vicious, angry boy when he left for college, embittered by his father's preference for Heathcliff. When Hindley returns, at his father's death, he cares nothing for the rest of his family, except to use them in exercising his newly acquired tyrannical power. Enraged that Heathcliff, in running around with Catherine, has called the outrage of the neighborhood on his head, Hindley cruelly beats Heathcliff and ostracizes him from family life, thus continuing the destruction of the family begun by his father with the introduction of Heathcliff. Although Heathcliff may have been partially responsible for the self-hatred Hindley evidences, it seems that he didn't need Heathcliff to help him lose his property and life. After his wife's death, Hindley becomes an insane alcoholic, almost killing his own child Hareton, and making Nelly accuse him of being worse than a heathen. Hindley is a parody of patriarchal oppression, making life hell for everyone while destroying himself and his property. Hareton is already a completely neglected child, wild, unkempt, and vicious, when Heathcliff returns to gamble with Hindley. Although Heathcliff plans to degrade Hareton as revenge against Hindley, he can hardly do worse than Hareton's father has already done, and Hareton can never be convinced that Heathcliff was not a good father to him. Hindley represents the self-destructiveness inherent in patrilinear society. Killing Hindley is "a piece of difficult work successfully executed" (144) for Heathcliff, yet at the same time Heathcliff probably saves Hareton's life and unwittingly allows the Earnshaw line to continue.

Hareton Earnshaw, Hindley's son, is the "natural" heir to Wuthering Heights, although the farm unnaturally descends to Heathcliff after Hindley's death. His mother Frances dies shortly after he is born, and his father cares nothing about him. Nelly nurses him and tries to protect him from Hindley's drunken fits of insanity, but even so he is almost killed when Hindley holds him over a second floor balcony and then accidentally drops him. Hareton is terrified of his father, and when Nelly leaves with Catherine upon her marriage, Hareton becomes a wild, neglected child, just as Heathcliff was after old Earnshaw's death. He hangs a litter of puppies, curses and throws things at Nelly, and is taught nothing. When Heathcliff comes to live at Wuthering Heights again, Hareton feels that Heathcliff protects him from his father, but this is all part of Heathcliff's plan to ruin Hareton and kill Hindley. After Hindley's death, Heathcliff continues to revenge himself on Hindley by degrading Hareton into a servant and a boor: "We'll see if any one tree won't grow as crooked as another, with the same wind to twist it" (144). But Hareton, unaware that he has been degraded, continues to see Heathcliff as a father figure, and Heathcliff cannot help admiring and sympathizing with Hareton, in whom he sees his younger self. Hareton doesn't brood on revenge and has a better character than Heathcliff had as a child, but whether this is hereditary or because Heathcliff is a better guardian than Hindley is up to the reader to decide.

Both Nelly and Heathcliff see in Hareton a diamond in the rough. Heathcliff acknowledges that Hareton is "gold put to the use of paving stones" (168), but Cathy sees only an illiterate boor for a long time. However, having no company but each other after Linton's death, they eventually become friends and lovers. Cathy teaches Hareton to read, and he eventually becomes a suitable husband for her. At the point of death, Heathcliff seems resigned to let Hareton and Cathy inherit both Wuthering Heights and Thrushcross Grange, and he may see his own story repeated with a happier ending in the young couple. Hareton has developed from a wild, abused child into a caring lover because he does not hold any grudges against Heathcliff for degrading him or Cathy for mocking his former ignorance.

Cathy's father Edgar Linton is presented less than sympathetically throughout the novel. We first see him weeping after a fight with his sister over a puppy. Then he is inadvertently enraging Heathcliff into throwing a pot of hot applesauce at him, causing Catherine to weep for the banishment of her first friend. He is just as vapid and foolish as Lockwood, and the fact that Lockwood admires Edgar Linton's portrait bespeaks the kinship he feels towards the dead man. Shocked that Catherine has told a lie, struck a servant, and then struck him, Edgar nevertheless proposes to her the same afternoon, even though the reason she won't let him leave is that "I should be miserable all night, and I won't be miserable for you!" (56). Nelly thinks Edgar must be "hopelessly stupid or a venturesome fool" to propose after that scene (60), but Edgar is infatuated by Catherine's very selfishness and temper. Their marriage is depicted as without conflict because Catherine is always given her own way. Catherine believes Edgar loves her so much that she "might kill him, and he wouldn't wish to retaliate" (76), but as soon as Linton objects to Heathcliff's return, Catherine is again scolding Edgar for being sulky and peevish rather than being "some living creature" who can keep her company (76). She despises his "weak nature" and calls him a "sucking leveret"—an unweaned hare—when he fears to fight Heathcliff hand to hand. Linton wins this battle, however, with a surprise blow and help from several of his employees, and he then tries to force Catherine to choose between him and Heathcliff. She claims his "veins are full of ice water" and begins to starve herself into a fever. Edgar is so upset by her condition that he almost fires Nelly for warning him about Heathcliff's kissing Isabella. After

Catherine's death, Edgar seems to die himself, as if he were only borrowing life from Catherine. When he sleeps beside her dead body, his "features were almost as death-like as those of the form beside him" (127). He becomes a complete recluse, giving up his office of magistrate and not even attending church. The only place he visits is Catherine's grave, and as he lies dying many years later, he confesses that he has often longed for his own death so that he can rejoin Catherine, even though he has seen her on her dying day in the arms of another man. Like his sister, he is often weak and foolish, even though he is also gentle, kind, and forgiving.

Isabella Linton, Edgar's sister and later Catherine's sister-in-law, is like her brother in many ways. She is "infantile in manners"; her education and social position have not prepared her for the world or imbued her with common sense. She refuses to believe that Heathcliff positively hates her, even though Catherine tells her that Heathcliff will "crush you like a sparrow's egg" and that she is no more fitted to be Heathcliff's wife than a canary is to fly in the park on a winter's day. Her social position as well as her relationship to Edgar make her despicable to Heathcliff, who sees her as "a strange repulsive animal, a centipede from the Indies" (82). She shows a strength of character by not complaining to her brother about Heathcliff's treatment of her, since she realizes that Heathcliff wants her to complain. Heathcliff finally lets her escape, realizing that he hates her so much that he will kill her otherwise, thus ruining his long range plans for revenge. By the time she runs away from Heathcliff, she has become almost as insane as the other inhabitants of the Heights, and if her son Linton's behavior is any indication of how she raised him, then the negative influence of her wealthy upbringing continued to have a deleterious effect into the next generation.

Linton Heathcliff, the child Isabella bears after she runs away, is a sickly, effeminate, whining, and completely self-centered child who strongly resembles his uncle Edgar Linton and looks nothing at all like Heathcliff, much to Heathcliff's chagrin. Heathcliff demands the child from Edgar on the very night of Linton's arrival at the Grange and laughs scornfully at the puny thing. He "felt his slender arms, and small fingers" (159) just as the witch does to Hansel and Gretel, and with just as evil intent. Left in a totally unsympathetic household, scorned by his father, Hareton, and Joseph, Linton becomes even more disagreeable. He delights in making fun of Hareton's ignorance, and when Hareton becomes angry and locks Linton out of the room, Linton screams with impotent fury, "I'll kill you, I'll kill you!" (191). As his illness worsens, he develops "the self-absorbed moroseness of a confirmed invalid," regarding the happiness of others as a personal insult (198). He degenerates still further when he helps lure Cathy into the house, knowing his father plans to imprison her there, because he fears for his own safety. His very worst traits are displayed after he is married to Catherine. He exults over now owning her property and being her master, and he doesn't allow her to escape even after their marriage until her desperation frightens him into it. Linton Heathcliff seems to represent the worst of the Lintons: he is spoiled, weak, peevish, and provoking. He longs to be cruel and exult in power over others but is too weak to do so.

Ellen (Nelly) Dean, the primary narrator, has lived her entire life at either Thrushcross Grange or Wuthering Heights. Her mother nursed Hindley, and so she grew up as Hindley's companion, much as Catherine and Heathcliff grow up together. But her mother was a servant, and she becomes a servant as soon as she is old enough to work. She never has any confusion about her social status, the way Heathcliff does. She is sometimes seen as a typical country woman with a limited understanding of the events she narrates, in the same way that Lockwood seems incapable of understanding everything he sees. More often, she is seen as the voice of reason, real life, pragmatism, and conventional Christianity. She never sympathizes with the first Catherine and tries to break her pride, showing that she is a supporter of the status quo, the patriarchal order of things. She disapproves of wayward girls and passionate women who want more than marriage, and she thinks Catherine is a spoiled and willful woman. When Nelly speaks of the battles between men, however, she always sympathizes with the victim at any particular time: Heathcliff when Hindley is oppressing him, but Hindley when Heathcliff comes back to ruin him, and Hareton when Heathcliff is keeping him in abject servitude, leading some to describe her as a mother figure. However, Nelly is sometimes seen as the primary cause of some of the trouble she narrates. She arranges the meeting between Heathcliff and the dying Catherine. She reminds Cathy of her promise to meet Linton Heathcliff and "obtained permission to order her out of doors" (201) when Cathy preferred to remain by her dying father's bedside, thus precipitating Cathy's imprisonment by Heathcliff.

While Nelly represents traditional Anglicanism, Joseph, the ancient servant who has served the Earnshaws for sixty years, is a fundamentalist Calvinist who delights in torturing everyone with long sermons, protracted blessings, and interminable services when the family cannot go to church. Nelly describes him as "the wearisomest, self-righteous pharisee that ever ransacked a Bible to rake the promises to himself, and fling the curses on his neighbors" (32). Joseph is partially responsible for turning old Earnshaw against his own children, by constantly pointing out their faults and encouraging him to "regard Hindley as a reprobate" (32). He is also responsible for Catherine and Heathcliff's aversion to any Christian heaven, since he makes them read religious tracts until they rebelliously throw the books away, Catherine vowing that she "hated a good book" (17). He encourages Hindley to persecute Heathcliff and

Catherine, but then thinks that Hindley deserves to be damned and destroyed by Heathcliff. His relationship to oppressive religion yoked with oppressive capitalism is symbolized by his covering his large Bible "with dirty bank-notes" (239) before passing them on to Heathcliff. He is a confirmed misogynist, despising and cursing Catherine, Isabella, Cathy, and Nelly, calling them witches and encouraging his masters to abuse them. Joseph caricatures all the oppressive forces of the sadistic and hypocritical social order that Brontë criticizes in this novel.

The primary narrator, Mr. Lockwood, remains unchanged by the violent, passionate events he narrates. The entire novel is Lockwood's diary, and thus all of the events come to the reader through Lockwood's consciousness. He is a wealthy, cultured young gentleman who, mistakenly thinking that he is a misanthropist, seeks solitude in the rough, isolated Yorkshire hills. However, he finds a real misanthropist like Heathcliff appalling and solitary confinement at Thrushcross Grange almost unbearable. While he is recuperating from a long illness, he entreats Nelly Dean to entertain him with the story of Wuthering Heights. He has conventional ideas about women and about religion. At one point, Nelly imagines that he could save Cathy from Heathcliff by marrying her, but he realizes that he is not the retiring type: "My home is not here. I'm of the busy world, and to its arms I must return" (195). How much Lockwood's perspective is meant to color the narrative is not clear. For example, has he really been visited by Catherine's ghost and, incapable of believing in ghosts, insisted on believing it was all a nightmare? His final pronouncement on "the sleepers in that quiet earth" surely lying peacefully under the benign sky is in stark contrast with the description of Heathcliff's death and of his and Catherine's ghosts haunting the countryside. His conventional, civilized point of view allows the reader to accept the violent, passionate, and highly unusual family history he narrates. His lack of passion aligns him with Edgar and Nelly as opposed to Catherine and Heathcliff.

THEMATIC ISSUES

Patriarchal oppression is one key thematic issue in the text. This oppression is represented by the male heads of families: Mr. Earnshaw senior, then Hindley Earnshaw, then Heathcliff, as well as the elder Mr. Linton and then Edgar Linton. It is also represented by the religious and legal structure of society: Catherine is constantly rebelling against Joseph's religious tyranny, while Isabella Linton and Cathy Linton Heathcliff are enslaved by a legal system highly injurious to women. Old Earnshaw has never approved of Catherine because of her high spirits and lack of ladylike manners. He grows more despotic and dissatisfied with her until his death, when his son Hindley takes over as a caricature of male despotism, demanding absolute respect and meting out cruel punishments. Catherine has scribbled her rage and rebelliousness in the margins of her Testament and tracts and throws one of Joseph's religious books into the dog kennel. Joseph and Hindley cannot keep Catherine in her place as effectively as Mr. Earnshaw, who would have "laced [her] properly" for her disobedience, but where whippings fail, Catherine is foiled by bonds of velvet and lace.

Mr. Linton the elder takes the wild Catherine into Thrushcross Grange and makes a lady out of her, while she is healing from her dog bite. For the first time, Catherine experiences some of the privileges of femininity in a patriarchal culture and is seduced into compliance. Her bond with Heathcliff is broken by her desire for the status and petty tyranny she enjoys as a guest at Thrushcross Grange, and later as its mistress. Only when Heathcliff returns, disguised as a gentleman to gain admittance into the Linton household, does Catherine realize the golden cage she has been lured into is a prison. The only way to escape it, to return to her former freedom, is through death.

At times the younger Cathy is a parody of refined upper-class womanhood, raised to do nothing and know nothing. When Heathcliff as her father-in-law tries to make her earn her keep, she refuses to do anything—on general principal. She insists on being an "idle jade" and doing nothing "except what I please" (24), which angers Heathcliff to no end. Later, she has Hareton tear up Joseph's currant and gooseberry bushes to plant a flower garden, destroying the practical and the necessary in favor of the frivolously decorative.

The theme of awakening sexuality associated with violence and death is also powerfully developed. The young Catherine and Heathcliff run to Thrushcross Grange to escape not only Hindley's tyranny but also his love-play with his new wife Frances. But Catherine is twelve years old, and though she may be disgusted by kissing and baby talk, she must inevitably become a woman. She loses her shoes in the marsh, is "soundly beaten" in the race by Heathcliff, and then is bitten by the Linton bulldog, whose tongue and lips form a grotesque phallic image. Losing her shoes symbolizes Catherine's sexual vulnerability: either Heathcliff will "soundly beat" her or she will be sexually initiated at the Grange. The Grange triumphs over Heathcliff, but Catherine's marriage to Edgar Linton results in her death while bearing Linton's child. Catherine is doomed to be murdered by adult sexuality, the same fate that befell Frances Earnshaw. Isabella Linton's desire for Heathcliff is sexual, dangerous, destructive, and almost deadly, blinding her to Heathcliff's faults and to his nefarious plan to abuse and degrade her as part of his revenge on Edgar. Catherine's daughter Cathy is tricked by her nascent love into marriage with Linton Heathcliff, whose speedy death suggests that Cathy's initiation into adult sexuality is yet to come. Her budding womanhood infuriates all the males at the Heights: Heathcliff, Joseph, and even Hareton Earnshaw, her future husband. They call her a "witch" in comparison to Lockwood's terms for her—"fairy" and "sprite." While the novel ends with Cathy's "taming" the degraded Earnshaw and he enchanted by her spell, this may not be a "happily-ever-after" ending but the beginning of another cycle of hatred and abuse. Heathcliff had also been enchanted by Catherine, but his feeling of being enchanted, bewitched, and haunted by a woman leads to his fury directed at all the world. The violent, hateful relationship between Cathy and Hareton that opens the novel may bode ill for their future happiness.

The theme of insubstantial, shifting, fluid identity is created partially by the dizzying repetition of names: different characters have very similar names. This swirl of names, which engenders Lockwood's nightmare, suggests that the characters represent forces rather than individuals, forces that combine, blow apart, and are recombined. Catherine Earnshaw wonders whether to become Catherine Heathcliff or Catherine Linton. She chooses Linton. Her daughter Catherine Linton becomes first Catherine Heathcliff and then, presumably, Catherine Earnshaw. Isabella names her son *Linton* Heathcliff, adding to the confusion. "Linton" may represent refined civilization, "Heathcliff" the inhuman force of nature, and "Earnshaw" violent, unrefined patriarchy.

The identity or thematic significance of Heathcliff presents a unique problem in literary criticism. Heathcliff has only one name, suggesting a primordial origin and a pure, uncombined nature. Many critics see Heathcliff as symbolizing a part of Catherine that she is forced, or chooses, to give up, but they differ on what exactly he symbolizes. Since they are parted when she is twelve, it may be that her initiation into womanhood requires that she leave behind her prepubescent, androgynous existence, shed her masculine, tomboy ways, and narrow herself down into a lady. This is a negative paring away of essential parts of the character in order to fit social stereotypes. Heathcliff has also been seen as the inner source of all creativity, that part of the self that is impervious to social claims. Catherine betrays her own creative soul when she turns to the social world of the Lintons and away from the asocial world of Heathcliff. Emily Brontë may have felt this way herself, since she hardly ever left home and made no friends outside of her family. The publication of her poems, and then of the novel, could have been seen by her as a fatal turning away from her inner source of life and art, toward the world of a reading public.

Love seems to be the central theme of *Wuthering Heights* to many readers, who remember it primarily as a great love story, and certainly it would be hard to point to more passionate characters than Heathcliff and Catherine. But their love is so passionate that it is cruel, sadistic, masochistic, and life destroying. Catherine is supremely, unself-consciously, uncalculatingly selfish, and Heathcliff is supremely and unremorsefully demanding and vengeful. Nelly notices "how much selfishness there is even in a love like Mr. Linton's, when he so regretted Catherine's blessed release!" (127). Yet Linton's love for Catherine is paltry and insipid compared to Heathcliff's, and it is Heathcliff's great love that can never forgive Catherine for betraying her own heart, or forgive anyone who has stood in its way. Catherine wishes Heathcliff were dead so they would never be parted, and Heathcliff does not refrain from visiting Catherine although he has been warned that she is very ill and may not be able to stand the shock. A great desire cannot be restrained by mere social conventions, physical pain, or even death. Brontë seems to believe, like William Blake, that "those who restrain desire, do so because theirs is weak enough to be restrained," and other similarities to Blake's "The Marriage of Heaven and Hell" are worth exploring. A great passion knows neither morality, consequences, nor limits: it is equivalent to the instinct of self-preservation, since the beloved is as essential to the lover's life as oxygen. The last scene between Catherine and Heathcliff is therefore supremely cruel and heartbreaking at the same time, for Catherine clings to Heathcliff as to life itself, never caring that he will be found by her husband, and Heathcliff savagely accuses her of killing herself and thereby killing him.

Revenge is also a central theme, and the plot may have been influenced by Jacobean revenge tragedies such as John Webster's *The Duchess of Malfi* (c. 1613). The plot of an evil, illegitimate younger brother scheming to deprive a legitimate older brother of his lands is reminiscent of Shakespeare's *King Lear* (1608), and it has been suggested that Edgar Linton's first name alludes to Edgar, Gloucester's elder, legitimate son in that tragedy. Since the entire revenge plot begins with a woman's infidelity, so to speak, shadows of Helen of Troy and the Greek myths and epics may also add to the resonance of the plot.

As in the Greek epics, women are simply helpless pawns in the wars between men, who think of them as possessions. Catherine seeks to avoid being objectified by marrying someone she can control. Similarly, Nelly tells Edgar not to worry if Cathy marries Linton since "he would not be beyond her control, unless she were extremely and foolishly indulgent" (195). Cathy seems attracted to Linton because she can treat him like a pet. But all the women characters find that marriage brings bondage and imprisonment. Women's desire for power within marriage is symbolized by Isabella Linton coveting Hindley's pistol: "A hideous notion struck me. How powerful I should be possessing such an instrument" (109). But Isabella rejects the opportunity to assist in Heathcliff's murder when offered the opportunity by Hindley, choosing to use her tongue as a weapon instead.

Brontë presents marriage as imprisonment for women partly because they leave their childhood home to enter the world of their spouse. The theme of feeling "not at home" anywhere but in one's childhood home is prevalent throughout the novel. Catherine dies wishing only that she could return to the home she had at Wuthering Heights before her father died. Isabella runs away from Wuthering Heights and would stay at the Grange, which she considers "my right home," except that she knows Heathcliff would follow her there and make life miserable for everyone (132). Just as Heathcliff imprisons Isabella at Wuthering Heights, he imprisons the younger Cathy to force her to marry Linton. While Cathy found it too easy to escape from the Grange, telling Nelly that it is not a prison, she finds it almost impossible to escape from the Heights, where she is actually imprisoned. Cathy is symbolically locked out of Thrushcross Grange, her rightful home, when Heathcliff accosts her and accuses her of breaking Linton's heart, convincing her that she must visit him or he will die. Being locked out makes Cathy vulnerable to Heathcliff's argument, which leads directly to her marriage with Linton Heathcliff. At her next visit with Linton, Cathy expresses the wish that Linton were her brother rather than her husband, because "people hate their wives, sometimes; but not their sisters and brothers, and if you were the latter, you would live with us, and papa would be as fond of you as he is of me" (182). If Linton were Cathy's brother, Cathy would not have to leave home to be with him.

Marriage is seen as a violent wrenching away from home, induced by temporary insanity or pity. Heathcliff tells Nelly that Isabella abandoned her family "under a delusion," imagining him "a hero of romance, and expecting unlimited indulgences from my chivalrous devotion" (116). Catherine seems to accept Edgar Linton's proposal out of pity for him and because she is under the delusion that marriage will not force her separation from Heathcliff. While Catherine actually gets almost unlimited indulgence from Edgar Linton, he insists on her complete break with Heathcliff and Wuthering Heights, her childhood home. Cathy is led by pity alone into the trap of marrying Linton, but perhaps her planned return to Thrushcross Grange with Hareton indicates better prospects for her second marriage. Emily Brontë was always miserable away from home, often becoming dangerously ill when away, and left as seldom as possible. Her primal need for home is evident in her fiction.

Women are sometimes seduced into leaving home to acquire a higher social standing, but elevated social class and wealth are associated with corruption. It is possible to read *Wuthering Heights* as social criticism, or even as an indictment of the class system and capitalism itself. Heathcliff feels that Catherine has rejected him only because he is poor and uneducated, but he leaves before he can hear that Catherine does not mean to abandon him. He returns, three years later, with money, education (or at least an educated appearance), and a determination to revenge himself on his enemies. He could not have achieved this revenge without money and polish. It is his ready money that seduces Hindley into allowing him into Wuthering Heights as a gambling partner. It is his polish that allows Isabella to become infatuated with him even though, as a child, she had been repelled by his dirty, bedraggled aspect. Money and education make Heathcliff powerful, but not better, and the novel implies that no one is made better by these acquisitions. Edgar Linton uses his money, in the form of his hired hands, to expel Heathcliff from the house, but later Heathcliff uses his own money to bribe Mr. Green the lawyer into not visiting Edgar Linton in time to allow him to change his will before he dies. Many critics see in *Wuthering Heights* a story of class conflict and read it as a fable of the violence and exploitation undergirding civilized society. The civilized Thrushcross Grange is protected by vicious bulldogs; the feather pillow on which Catherine lies dying has required the death of countless birds. But money is also seen as breeding weaklings and fools. Heathcliff, having overcome great adversity, is a much stronger man than Hindley. Yet Hindley's son Hareton, similarly reduced to servitude, is a much stronger man than Linton, Heathcliff's son, who has been raised genteelly.

Emily Brontë rejects many of the values of traditional society, including the traditional images of heaven and hell. The many references to heaven and hell show that Brontë inverts the meaning of heaven and hell just as William Blake had done: heaven is a prison ruled by a tyrant, and hell is creative energy freed from restraint. Catherine and Heathcliff both reject the traditional heaven that Nelly Dean looks forward to. Catherine dreams that the angels threw her out of heaven because she was so miserable there, and flung her back onto the heath at Wuthering Heights, where she wept for joy. Heathcliff sends Edgar Linton to heaven in his curses, instead of to hell (87), and nearing death, states, "I have nearly attained my heaven; and that of others is altogether unvalued and uncoveted by me!" (253).

In her poetry as well as in *Wuthering Heights*, Brontë constructs her own idea of heaven, and of life after death. Half of *Wuthering Heights* takes place after the heroine's death, but Heathcliff believes that Catherine's ghost still walks the earth—only her body is in the grave, not her spirit. Lord David Cecil, an influential early critic of the novel, writes that Brontë believes in "the immortality of the soul *in this world*" (149), not in a supernatural way but as if it were natural for the disembodied human spirit, finally freed from its prison house the body, to exist in nature. The dying Catherine longs to "escape into that glorious world and to be always there: not seeing it dimly through tears, and yearning for it through the walls of an aching heart: but really with it, and in it" (124). For Catherine, as for Emily Brontë, the world itself is more beautiful than any heaven could possibly be, if only we could commune with it fully, without the impediment of the body. If Heathcliff and Catherine do "walk" the moors after their deaths, they have achieved their heaven, which is not Nelly's and certainly not Joseph's heaven but their own.

HISTORICAL/SOCIAL-CULTURAL CONTEXTS

The plot of *Wuthering Heights* depends in large measure on the laws of England in and around 1800. The younger Cathy marries two of her first cousins. This had for centuries been an accepted practice among the landed gentry and aristocracy, as it kept the wealth and estates of a family intact. The elder Catherine ponders marrying her foster brother Heathcliff, and while many critics have seen an implied incest theme, her marriage to Heathcliff would not have been legal incest then or now, especially since Heathcliff was never adopted into the family. Victor Frankenstein, in Mary Shelley's novel, is similarly engaged to and marries a girl his family has raised since she was a child.

Heathcliff's revenge upon the Earnshaws and Lintons consists of acquiring their lands, movable property, and women. The law of entail, which plays an important role in many other British novels, including *Pride and Prejudice*, dictates how an estate is passed down through the generations. In his influential article, "The Structure of Wuthering Heights," the critic C. P. Sanger shows how Brontë used the laws of entail, inheritance, and marriage effectively and accurately. Thrushcross Grange is entailed to Edgar Linton as the male heir, but if Edgar has no male heir, the estate passes to Isabella rather than to Edgar's daughter. Edgar Linton's father had secured his estate "to his own daughter, instead of his son's" (127). Because Edgar Linton has no son, the estate entails to Isabella rather than to Cathy, and to Isabella's son Linton after her death. However, Linton Heathcliff has possession of the estate only during his lifetime. At his death, it would not pass to his father Heathcliff but to Cathy, as she is the last surviving heir of the Lintons.

Heathcliff's possession of Thrushcross Grange is technically illegal, but Cathy does not have the power or money to regain her estate. His possession of Wuthering Heights is more straightforward. Being a farm and not an estate, it was probably not entailed but owned outright by old Earnshaw, and it descended to his only son as the heir-at-law, since Earnshaw probably did not leave a will. Hindley mortgages the entire property, lands and goods, to Heathcliff, who becomes the "mortgagee in possession" of the farm and all its property until an heir can pay off the mortgage. Hindley will inherit this property and any remaining debts on it at Heathcliff's death, whether or not Heathcliff leaves a will, since he has not held it long enough to acquire it outright as payment of the mortgages.

The laws of marriage enable Heathcliff to obtain not only possession of Isabella and of his son, but of all Cathy's movable property. Before the Married Woman's Property Act of 1882, a married woman, all her goods, and all her children born in wedlock were the legal property of her husband under the common law doctrine of "coverture." A married woman had no legal existence.

Her husband was legally responsible for her, so he could punish her within reason if she disobeyed him and could force her to return home if she left. If a wife, such as Isabella Linton, separated from her husband and set up a separate residence, she could be forced to return, or every item of personal property and money she possessed could be confiscated by her husband and any children she took with her could be demanded at will by her husband. Isabella is fortunate that Heathcliff does not demand Linton before her death, since according to common law, a father owned his children and could "take them from [the mother] and dispose of them as he thought fit" (Perkin 15). Fathers were known to spirit away the children to torture and punish their wives in cases of acrimonious marriage or separation.

The only grounds for a wife to seek a legal separation was to claim extreme physical cruelty, and Heathcliff promises to keep his physical and mental torture of Isabella within the limits of the law, to prevent her from having any legal grounds to leave him. Whatever personal property Isabella possesses becomes Heathcliff's when they marry, and similarly, all of Cathy's personal property becomes Linton's when she marries him. Both Linton and his father cruelly drive this point home by tearing a locket from Cathy's neck, stealing her mother's portrait, and grinding her father's portrait into the floor, to prove that she doesn't even own the clothing and jewelry on her own body. Nor, coincidentally, does she own her own body at this point, but since Linton is too sickly to consummate the marriage, Heathcliff symbolically rapes her by brutally striking her on the face, making her mouth fill with blood and leaving her unable to talk.

Heathcliff forces or convinces Linton to make a will leaving all of his personal property to his father, effectively making Cathy a beggar after her husband's death, since at her marriage everything she has becomes her husband's, and Linton has been forced or convinced to leave everything to his father in his will. At this point, Cathy's closest living relative appears to be her father-in-law, making it probable that Heathcliff becomes Cathy's legal guardian as well. But Emily Brontë makes it clear that whether or not Heathcliff is Cathy's legal guardian, or legally possesses Thrushcross Grange, he is effectively possessor of both estate and girl, since there is no representative of the "law" able or willing to interfere on Cathy's behalf.

A married woman's lack of legal rights was of great concern to all the Brontë sisters. Anne Brontë's *The Tenant of Wildfell Hall* is about a cruel, alcoholic father who abuses his son, forcing his wife to "steal" their child and live incognito, thus breaking the law that held that the child is indisputably his father's property. When Charlotte Brontë married the Reverend Nichols at the age of thirty-eight, she was already a famous novelist making a good income, and she bitterly resented the fact that all her copyrights and income automatically became the property of her husband upon her marriage.

LITERARY DEVICES AND CRAFT

Wuthering Heights has long been considered a powerfully original creation, owing less to the literary tradition than to the subconscious mind of Emily Brontë. However, in its narrative structure, it does have precedents. The layers of narrators, with the outermost narrator most closely resembling the supposed reader, is a device used most memorably in Mary Shelley's *Frankenstein* (1818). These layers of narrators—Captain Walton/Victor Frankenstein/the monster, or Mr. Lockwood/Nelly Dean/documents written by Catherine Earnshaw, Isabella Linton, etc.—help the reader accept the "reality" of otherwise unbelievable or at least very unusual events. If Mr. Lockwood, an unimaginative but educated man of the world, and Nelly Dean, an earthy, staid, ordinary servant, relate these events to us as real, then we must accept them as happening in the "real" world, near a village in Yorkshire, England, at a certain historical time.

This type of narrative strategy prevents the story from being recounted in strictly chronological order, since the outermost narrator, in order to appear objective and normal, cannot have been observing these unusual events happening over time. If he had, his objectivity or sanity would also be suspect. Instead, he witnesses a small part of the action and hears the rest narrated to him. However, layers of first-person narrators also make it hard to know who, if anyone, speaks for the author's point of view. Most readers assume that Brontë does not sympathize with either Lockwood's or Nelly Dean's pragmatic, conventional view of the world. But readers differ on how sympathetically to interpret Heathcliff and Catherine.

The novel is also characterized by intense polarities that have been variously interpreted. Wuthering Heights and Thrushcross Grange seem to present totally different ways of life. According to critic David Cecil, the Heights represents the principle of storm—harsh, ruthless, wild, dynamic, while the Grange represents the principle of calm—gentle, merciful, passive, and tame (146). Neither is inherently good or bad, but they are opposites, and the marriage of storm and calm—Catherine and Edgar—results in a catastrophe. Catherine constrasts herself to Edgar by saying his veins have ice water while hers are burning and that she has no more business marrying Edgar than going to heaven. Edgar Linton and Heathcliff present opposing types, as do Catherine and Isabella, while Catherine and Heathcliff are presented as being so alike that they are, in fact, each other, and therefore their separation is a catastrophe for both.

Wuthering Heights is almost always read as a highly symbolic novel. The symbolic use of windows and doors, which separate the inside, or normal, social life from the outside, or wild, amoral, inhuman nature, was first pointed out by literary critic Dorothy Van Ghent. The ghost of Catherine tries to get in the window during Lockwood's nightmare, while Heathcliff, imprisoned in the material world, calls to the ghost from the window. Heathcliff and Catherine look into the civilized Linton household through a window, the dying Catherine throws open a window to find her way back to her true home through death, and the window by Heathcliff's corpse is open, indicating that he has escaped the civilized material world through the window, back into primordial nature.

Dreams are almost always symbolic, and Catherine's dream of being thrown out of heaven seems to prefigure the rest of the novel. Her memory of finding a nest of baby lapwing skeletons has also been seen as highly symbolic. Because Heathcliff is the one who set a trap over the nest, it may symbolize Heathcliff's savage and murderous nature, but because both Catherine and Heathcliff are orphans, "abandoned" by their parents and the world, the baby skeletons may also symbolize their condition in the world. Perhaps, however, the skeletons symbolize everyone's condition in the world, where we are all left abandoned and starving, longing desperately for union with and nourishment from heaven and earth.

The relationship between Catherine and Heathcliff has often been seen as a symbolic relationship between two forces rather than two characters. Their attraction to each other seems primordial, irresistible, and tragic. While it is possible to view their common bond as having been forged by rebellion against Hindley's oppression, it is also possible to see Catherine's betrayal of Heathcliff as a betrayal of something basic and essential within herself that leads directly to her self-annihilation.

ALTERNATIVE PERSPECTIVE: JUNGIAN CRITICISM

Carl Gustav Jung (1875–1961) was Sigmund Freud's most famous pupil, and therefore Jungian criticism is a type of psychoanalytic criticism. Like Freud (see chapter 6), Jung, who was born and lived his entire life in Switzerland, trained as a psychiatrist and studied the severely mentally ill. However, while Freud believed that the unconscious mind consisted of sexual and aggressive desires repressed by the conscious mind, Jung came to believe that below that personal unconscious mind was a collective unconscious, formed over millions of years of human experience, which would explain the similar myths and symbols found in vastly different cultures separated by time and space. The collective unconscious contains "archetypes" or structures that are filled in by actual experience. Some of these archetypes are parts of the self: the mask, the shadow, the anima or animus, and the spirit.

For example, the Shadow archetype is the primordial memory of experiencing our dark, unconscious fears and desires. These illogical, chaotic, primordial fears and desires can be represented in literature by images of the wilderness. When Hansel and Gretel enter the dark woods, they leave logic and civilization behind and enter a fearful, dangerous, evil, illogical, uncivilized place. Jesus spent forty days and forty nights in the wilderness, wrestling with Satan. People tend to see their shadows in others—they project their dark side onto another person or people who are dark, dangerous, wild, evil, or exotic. Thus Satan himself is a personification of the shadow, the enemy of man who tempts him into the darker side of his nature.

Wuthering Heights seems to reverberate with some mythic, timeless intensity, and therefore we may suspect that it embodies some archetypal pattern or makes particular some oft-recurring human experience that occurs because we are human, not because we live in a particular time or place. Heathcliff seems to embody some of the archetypal qualities of the shadow. He is of unknown parentage, a stranger introduced into a closed society, a "cuckoo" in the nest, as many critics have pointed out, who destroys the legitimate children. The cuckoo lays her eggs in another bird's nest, and after the host bird has hatched the eggs and fed the chicks, the cuckoo chick, stronger than the others, throws the other chicks out of the nest. Heathcliff may represent the dark, animalistic side of the Earnshaws that is released at his arrival. His name, a combination of "heath" and "cliff," reinforces this interpretation. The heath, in *Wuthering Heights*, always represents the wilderness, where Cathy and Heathcliff roam wild and free, unrestrained by Catherine's father or brother. A cliff is also part of a wild natural scene, enticing and dangerous as the same time. Catherine's daughter Cathy longs to climb up to Penistone Crags to see the fairy caves. Nelly tries to dissuade her, but Cathy cannot resist the temptation and finally breaks the bonds of civilization, leaps over the hedge of Thrushcross Grange on her pony, and rides toward the forbidden fairy caves. Before she arrives, she will meet the shadow, personified in Heathcliff.

Another powerful archetype is the anima or animus. For Jung, the human self is born whole but easily becomes fragmented by society as it matures. The anima, or feminine side of the male self, may be repressed in a society that values masculine males, and the animus, or male side of the female self, may similarly be repressed in a society that values feminine females. Since Heathcliff and Catherine so often say that they *are* each other's souls or lives—"Nelly, I am Heathcliff," is one of the most famous lines in all literature—it is possible to read the forced feminization of Catherine (at the hands of the Lintons and Frances Earnshaw) as a violent splitting of the self that causes emotional turmoil and physical illness. Heathcliff is similarly split off from his feminine self when his resolve to "be good" is crushed by Hindley's cruelty, and his need to be protected and nourished by Catherine is denied. He becomes a "fierce, piti-less, wolfish" man completely cut off from his own anima. The animus is often represented as a dark, handsome, mysterious, and exotic stranger who has a strong animal magnetism irresistible to a woman. Neither Catherine, Isabella, nor even Cathy seem to be able to resist Heathcliff's magnetism.

For the critic Stevie Davies, *Wuthering Heights* is about a female human soul seeking its lost, male counterpart, and it is possible to see Catherine and Heathcliff's desire for each other as a desire for something essential to psychic health in the self. Both of them long to return to a childhood wholeness they experienced together, before sexual maturity and the expectations of society separated them. While Jung felt that the goal of life was to achieve a harmoni-ous balance of all the elements of the psyche, he believed that this was ex-tremely difficult to do. Catherine and Heathcliff never approach a harmonious balance. Instead, they suffer great psychic pain and cause others pain because an essential part of their psyche has not been integrated but instead has been vi-olently severed or repressed.

However, Catherine's death is also a rebirth—her spirit is released from the bondage of marriage and motherhood, and she will meet Heathcliff again, when they are both spirits, to wander the heaths. The archetype of death and rebirth is also a powerful motif encountered in many religions as well as in folk tales, fairy tales, and literature. The archetype of death and rebirth offers hope that we can be reborn, or regain a paradise once lost. The death and resurrec-tion of Christ, as well as the birth of the Christ child that Christians celebrate every year, is the most resonant rebirth archetype in the Western world. Catherine and Heathcliff both die but are reborn into a spirit world that is their paradise, where they will never be parted from each other.

The syzygy, or divine couple, is another powerful archetype that represents the integration of different parts of the psyche. Sometimes represented by an enchanted castle with a king and a queen, it signifies the joining of the outer and inner life of the soul, the reconciliation of warring opposites into a power-ful union. Not only are Catherine and Heathcliff joined in death, but more sig-nificantly, the warring houses of Earnshaw and Linton are to be united with the marriage of Hareton and Cathy. Nature and civilization, lower class and upper class, animal and spiritual, male and female are to achieve harmonious union, ending decades of strife and bloodshed.

Jungian criticism may help to explain the emotional resonance and power of *Wuthering Heights*. Many critics feel that Emily Brontë had an unusually open access to subconscious emotions and desires. She insisted on following her own path in life, listened much more intently than most to her own inner voice, and kept herself amazingly untainted from all worldly concerns and affairs. Her intense concentration on the inner life allowed her to tap into and use powerful collective memory traces more fully and purely; her genius and unconcern with convention allowed her to flesh out these archetypes with more emotional intensity than any other British novelist before or since.

4

Jane Eyre
(1847)

Charlotte Brontë's most popular novel and one of the most widely read classics of English literature, *Jane Eyre* was an immediate best-seller upon its publication in 1847, although the novel also attracted some negative criticism. While most early Victorian readers liked the emotional intensity, some, like well-known author, art historian, and literary critic Elizabeth Rigby, felt that the novel was dangerously unchristian, rebellious, or even revolutionary in its critique of religious hypocrisy, upper-class prerogatives, and a stratified social order. Some felt that the novelist was not in control of her narrative or was writing a veiled autobiography.

Twentieth-century critics such as Adrienne Rich, Sandra Gilbert, and Mary Poovy have found the novel to be refreshingly feminist, advocating as it does a woman's right to the pursuit and attainment of happiness as she understands it. Others, however, criticize the novel's tacit acceptance of racism, imperialism, and the stratified social order. But however they interpret it, readers and critics have continued to find *Jane Eyre* a compelling narrative, and it remains one of the most popular English novels ever written.

PLOT DEVELOPMENT

Jane Eyre is a bildungsroman because it is about the growth and education of the main character. The plot can be neatly divided into the five locations where Jane lives and learns important lessons about life: Gateshead, Lowood,

Thornfield, Moor House, and Ferndean. When the novel opens, Jane Eyre is a ten-year-old orphan living at Gateshead Hall with her wealthy Aunt Reed, who resents having to raise the poor orphan. Jane's cousin John Reed, the fourteen-year-old heir of the estate, is allowed to physically and verbally abuse Jane, while his sisters Eliza and Georgiana are treated like ladies. Jane is constantly reminded that she is an unwanted and unloved dependent. When she finally dares to strike back at John Reed, she is locked in the Red Room where Mr. Reed died and left there for the night without a candle, despite her desperate pleas for help. She suffers a fit, brought on by fright and an overactive imagination fired by the ghost stories told by the servants. Mrs. Reed sends for the local apothecary, or pharmacist, since she won't waste money on a doctor just for Jane. The apothecary sees that Jane is the victim of physical and psychological abuse, and tactfully suggests to Mrs. Reed that Jane be sent to school.

Mrs. Reed summons Mr. Brocklehurst, a minister who runs Lowood, a charity school for orphans. During Mr. Brocklehurst's examination of Jane, Mrs. Reed says that Jane is deceitful and troublesome. That night, after Brocklehurst's departure, the tiny orphan accuses Mrs. Reed of gross mistreatment and gains a small victory over the discomposed widow. At Gateshead, or the beginning of her journey, Jane has learned to abhor being a dependent, someone "less than a servant" (9) who, because she is unwanted, unloved, and does not earn her keep, has no right to anything at all. She realizes that she must love herself if she is to survive, but she also learns that her passionate outbursts of aggrieved selfhood can lead to banishment and even madness, as they had in the Red Room.

At Lowood Jane learns how to control her violent emotions, but she and the other students suffer terribly from the inedible and scanty food, the bitter winters, and the sadistic discipline. Here she meets Helen Burns, an intelligent, sensitive, and pious fourteen-year-old who meekly submits to the worst injustices. Asked how she can submit so passively, Helen reminds Jane that Christ asks us to turn the other cheek. Miss Temple, the head teacher, is kind to Helen and to Jane, but she can do little to improve the girls' living conditions. The same year that a typhus epidemic kills almost half the girls in the school, who have been weakened by the inedible food and bitter cold, Helen Burns dies of consumption, known today as tuberculosis. Helen is going "home," as she, like Jane, is homeless on this earth, but Jane is not willing to let go of the world and has no clear conception of heaven at this time.

After the typhus epidemic, the school is moved to a new, unspecified location. Jane continues on as student for eight years, then as teacher for two years, quite content under the serene and benevolent influence of Miss Temple. But when Miss Temple leaves the school to marry a clergyman, Jane finds her old spirit of restlessness rising. She is barely eighteen years old when she decides to better her condition and see more of the world by hiring herself out as a governess. Although Jane has learned to govern her emotions, she cannot follow Helen Burns's example of a passionate spirit's self-immolation. Her will to live and her indignation at injustice are too strong.

By controlling her passions, Jane has become a lady, as Bessie, one of Mrs. Reed's servants, tells her during an unexpected visit. From Bessie, Jane learns that her father's brother had come to see if he could find her seven years ago, that John Reed is very dissipated, and that Eliza and Georgiana hate and despise each other.

Jane's next school for the soul is at Thornfield Hall. Her advertisement in a regional newspaper yields one offer of employment, to tutor one child, Adèle Varens. She is the daughter of a French opera dancer, Céline Varens, whom the master of Thornfield, Edward Fairfax Rochester, had once loved passionately but who had betrayed him. Mrs. Fairfax, the housekeeper, insists there are no ghosts or legends of ghosts surrounding Thornfield, even though the isolated, half-abandoned, and gothic features of the house seem to suggest one. When Mrs. Fairfax takes Jane up to the third floor, to exit onto the roof and observe the view, Jane hears an eerie, hopeless, lunatic laugh. Mrs. Fairfax insists that it is only Grace Poole, a woman hired to sew for the household whose room is on the third floor. The plot now takes on some gothic characteristics: a spooky castlelike mansion, possibly haunted, with dangerous inhabitants.

Out walking one day, Jane assists a rider who has suffered a fall from his horse, and learns only later that she has assisted the master of Thornfield. Jane feels a natural affinity for her gloomy, moody employer. The gothic and romantic tensions of the plot heighten when Jane hears her doorknob being tried one night and hears a strange laugh outside her door. Frightened, she opens the door and sees smoke billowing out of her master's room down the hall. She rushes in and finds Rochester asleep on his burning bed. She douses him with water until he wakes. He runs up to the third floor, returns in depressed spirits, and instructs Jane to tell no one of what has happened. But he won't let her go until his looks, words, and actions have conveyed more than mere gratitude for her saving his life.

Jane realizes that she loves Rochester and that he may love her, but when she awakes the next morning he is gone. He returns a few weeks later with a houseful of guests, including the beautiful and accomplished Blanche Ingram, who everyone assumes is a perfect match for Rochester, despite their difference in age. Jane is mortified and chastises herself severely for ever thinking that she—a lowly, poor, unconnected governess—could ever have attracted the master of an estate. Forced to accompany Adèle to the drawing room for several weeks, Jane comes to realize that Blanche Ingram is shallow and proud, haughty and heartless. Blanche flirts with Rochester but does not love him;

moreover, Jane believes that Rochester does not love Blanche. Theirs will be the typical marriage of convenience, a consolidation of wealth and power, not a coming together of hearts and spirits.

The romantic tension is heightened when Rochester, disguised as a gypsy fortune-teller, tries to pressure Jane into admitting her love for him and her jealousy over seeing his courting of Blanche. When Rochester drops his disguise, after hinting that Jane has only to reach out her hand to find happiness, she informs him that a Mr. Mason from Spanishtown in Jamaica has come to visit him. Rochester is terribly shaken, but he meets Mr. Richard Mason and gives him a room.

The gothic tensions of the plot heighten when a terrible insane screaming is heard that night from the third floor above Jane's room. Rochester summons Jane to a third-floor chamber to take care of Mr. Mason, who has been violently attacked and is almost dying from fright and loss of blood. Rochester tells Mason not to talk to Jane on fear of his life, but the doctor summoned to tend to Mr. Mason's wounds notices that one is a bite, and Mason raves about how the creature said she would drink his blood. Rochester quickly and quietly escorts Mason out of the house and out of the country before anyone else has awakened the next morning, but Jane hears Mason plead to Rochester to take care of her and treat her well. Who is the madwoman in the attic? Why does she have so much power over Rochester?

Soon after, Jane is called to Mrs. Reed's deathbed. Afraid to die without repenting of a wrong she has done Jane, Mrs. Reed confesses that Jane's uncle, her father's brother, had come looking for her, saying that he wished to adopt Jane and make her his heir. She had told Mr. Eyre that Jane was dead, but now she gives Jane her uncle's letter. The orphan is closer to discovering her identity and true family.

Upon her return to Thornfield, Jane is waylaid by Rochester on one of her evening walks and discovers that she, not Miss Ingram, is Rochester's intended bride. He had been trying to arouse Jane's jealousy by courting Miss Ingram, who was only interested in his fortune. As soon as Jane finally accepts Rochester's proposal, a sudden thunderstorm forces them indoors. The next morning Jane learns that the great old chestnut tree under which they were sitting had been cleft in two by a bolt of lightning the night before. An important symbol, this tree cleft in two has been variously interpreted as predicting Jane's separation from Rochester, warning Jane about the destructive nature of electrifying passion, or as symbolizing Rochester's marriage to Bertha, to whom he is still legally tied.

The plot intensifies when, on the night preceding Jane's wedding day, she confides to Rochester that a strange and horrible woman had crept into her room in the middle of the night, torn her wedding veil in two, and stomped upon it. Jane relates that she passed out from terror for only the second time in her life (the first was in the Red Room). Rochester assures her that the woman was Grace Poole, but it was in fact Bertha Mason, the madwoman in the attic. Bertha hates Rochester and has tried to kill him, but she doesn't harm Jane. Is she warning Jane that her marriage will be bigamous, or, in reliving her hatred of the married state by tearing the veil, warning Jane that imprisonment and madness may result from marrying a powerful man?

At the private wedding ceremony a stranger, who turns out to be Mr. Mason's attorney, discloses that Rochester has a wife now living—imprisoned in his attic. Rochester, angry and desperate that his plans to commit bigamy have been stymied, takes everyone to meet the mad Bertha Mason. Like Miss Ingram, Bertha is full of "animal health and vigor" but the animal has prevailed over the human. Her vices have driven her to the insanity inherent in her ancestry (her "non-British" ancestry, as her mother was a Creole).

That night, Rochester implores Jane to be his nominal wife. He explains how he was tricked into marrying Bertha by his father and brother, simply because she was wealthy. After his brother and father's death in the course of four years, Rochester is left an even richer man, but he is prevented from divorcing his intolerable wife because she has been declared insane by the doctors, her insanity the result of her debauchery. His love, his despair, and his anguish move her, but Jane uses her last strength to resist becoming his mistress. She realizes that he holds his former mistresses in contempt, and she is either too religious and moral to accept such a proposal, or too frightened that such a union would crush the life and spirit out of her and destroy his love and esteem for her as well. Instead, she obeys a trancelike dream she has after her conversation with Rochester: the moon, or Nature personified, tells her, "my daughter, flee temptation," and she answers, "Mother, I will." She sneaks away from Rochester's house early the next morning, in agony over *his* possible suffering, not her own. All her money gets her as far as a distant hamlet, Whitcross, where she spends several miserable days without food or shelter. At the point of death, Jane is taken in by St. John Rivers, the local minister. The cottage where St. John lives is called Moor House, or Marsh End.

At Marsh End, Jane finally meets friends with "perfect congeniality of tastes, sentiments, and principles" and feels that she has finally found a family. St. John's sisters Mary and Diana are entirely sympathetic to her character and disposition. The fairy tale quality of the plot is heightened when Jane discovers that Mary, Diana, and St. John are her cousins, and that she has been left a fortune by her unknown uncle in Madiera. Jane continues to work in the village school and shares the legacy equally with her cousins, but St. John soon reveals his plan that Jane accompany him to India as a missionary's wife. Jane again must resist the tyranny of a strong-willed man: "I was tempted to cease struggling with him—to rush down the torrent of his will into the gulf of his existence, and there lose my own" (368).

Jane is about to submit but begs God to show her the path. Her plea for guidance is answered not by St. John's God but by that "nature" that had previously told her to "flee temptation" when Rochester urged her to become his mistress. Jane hears Rochester's voice calling her name, and finds the strength to break free of St. John's will and rush out into the night. No Rochester is there, but the supernatural experience makes Jane decide to find out conclusively what has happened to Rochester before annihilating herself by marrying St. John. She takes a journey to Thornfield, but finds it a charred ruin. She learns that Bertha Mason is dead, having set the house on fire and committed suicide, and that Rochester is blind, maimed, and living at Ferndean, another one of his properties, in gloomy solitude.

Ferndean, Rochester's isolated, unglamorous country house, is the end of Jane's journey. Rochester can barely believe that his little Jane has come back to him and that she would want to stay with him now, in his wretched condition. "I love you better now when I can really be useful to you than I did in your state of proud independence, when you disdained every part but the giver and protector," says Jane to the blinded Rochester. Whether her retreat into the isolation of Ferndean is positive or negative is up to the reader to decide. "Reader, I married him," the narrator Jane tells us but ends the narrative itself with a letter she receives from the dying St. John Rivers, an ending that has puzzled and fascinated readers and critics. Has Jane refused salvation for mere earthly happiness, or has she found a salvation of her own better fitted for her soul? Has she completely betrayed her feminist principles, or have they allowed her to triumph?

CHARACTER DEVELOPMENT

Jane Eyre is a small, underdeveloped, physically unattractive ten-year-old child when we meet her at Aunt Reed's, but she is intelligent, sensitive, and highly aware of her position as a social outcast in the Reed family. She has always submitted to John Reed's physical and mental abuse, knowing that she had no allies in the Reed household, but a spirit of rebellion rises in her when, after throwing a book at her, John threatens to hit her again. Her spirit of righteous indignation again rises when Mrs. Reed accuses her of being a liar in front of Mr. Brocklehurst. For the first time she accuses Mrs. Reed of being unjust and cruel. Even as a small child, she has decided that she must speak out against injustice, even if it means further punishment. From an abused and neglected child, she begins her development into a strong-willed, independent woman, able to bear loneliness and social ostracism.

However, this cycle of total submission followed by total revolt will be characteristic of Jane throughout the novel. "I know no medium: I never in my life have known any medium in my dealings with positive, hard characters, antagonistic to my own, between absolute submission and determined revolt. I have always faithfully observed the one, up to the very moment of bursting, sometimes with volcanic vehemence, into the other" (352). She will similarly seem to submit to Rochester's plan for her life until her headlong flight from Thornfield without money or belongings. She will submit completely to St. John's expectations until she finally revolts when he insists on a loveless marriage.

Jane's earlier revolts had a passionate, self-destructive character: "A ridge of lighted heath, alive, glancing, devouring, would have been a meet emblem of my mind when I accused and menaced Mrs. Reed: the same ridge, black and blasted after the flames are dead, would have represented as meetly my subsequent condition" (32). A fire of anger and resentment burns within Jane, but this same fire is her passion for life and freedom. She must learn to control the fire so that it isn't extinguished, as it would be if she were to submit totally, and so that it doesn't burn out of control, destroying herself and others.

At Lowood, Jane is most influenced by Helen Burns and Miss Temple. Helen Burns, like Jane, is intelligent and passionate, but unlike Jane, she has complete control over her passions. Helen is an excellent Christian because she has learned to love her enemies, but to do this she must despise herself. She looks for release through death from a miserable life of abuse and scorn, instead of opposing injustice in this life. Helen's last name, "Burns," symbolizes the way she burns within, and because the fire is never allowed to escape, she self-immolates on the altar of Christian charity. Jane later tells Rochester that she has no intention of being "hurried away in a suttee" like an Indian widow (240), or sacrificing her life for anyone or anything. Jane is very grateful for Helen's friendship and support, but she cannot stop feeling indignant at injustice. Jane wants to live, and in order to live, she feels a person must at times assert her own rights over those of others.

Miss Temple, like Helen Burns, is in total control of her emotions. A tender-hearted and generous person, Miss Temple quietly tries to improve the living conditions for the girls, but she will never demand change or accuse Mr. Brocklehurst or the slovenly cook. She is not burning inside like Helen but is cool and white as marble. The fire within her "temple" has been extinguished. Her actions, like Helen's, seem exemplary of the Christian virtues of temperance and mildness, but it is possible that a stronger will to do the *right* thing rather than the *good* thing would have produced changes before the typhus epidemic made the conditions at Lowood public knowledge. Jane learns self-control and peace of mind by imitating Miss Temple in order to earn Miss Temple's love, but she has not let the fire within her be totally extinguished. When Miss

Temple leaves, Jane rejects both Helen Burns and Miss Temple's examples, not because she doesn't admire them, but because her desire to be true to herself is too strong.

At Thornfield, Jane's outer self-control is severely tested. She realizes that she has fallen in love with Rochester and can do nothing to make herself stop loving him. She exhibits self-control when Rochester, disguised as a gypsy, attempts to get a confession of love out of her, but Rochester is not fooled by Jane's outer calmness: she is no temple, no marble monument to a god, but is herself a living, desiring soul, and it is her own central being that she values and seeks to preserve above all other earthly or heavenly goals.

Jane exhibits her outer self-control and inner sense of self-worth when she returns to Gateshead, to the deathbed of Mrs. Reed, as a stronger and more self-assured young lady. She is no longer mortified by the affectations and snubs of Eliza and Georgiana, because she has learned to value herself. She has been tested and found herself not brittle, but strong. She also has a secret hope and a secret love that support her.

Jane stands firm during her engagement to Rochester, refusing to become his harem girl. She plans to keep on working as Adèle's governess even after she and Rochester are married so that she can retain her own sense of self-worth. She also wants to avoid having her new identity as "Mrs. Rochester" completely subsume her present identity as Jane Eyre. Rochester is like a forest fire that will consume the smaller flame of Jane's life and identity. His will is too strong, and Jane's dependent economic position makes her weak. Rochester showers Jane with jewels and insists he will make a fine lady out of her, despite her appearance, her background, and her wishes, and Jane so longs for a balance of power that she writes to her unknown uncle Mr. Eyre, who had once expressed a desire to make her his heir.

When Jane discovers at the very altar that Rochester is already married, she must decide whether or not to become Rochester's mistress. There is no earthly reason to deny Rochester's plan, but Jane is warned by Nature to "flee temptation." Jane must resist the temptation to succumb to her sensual and sexual desires outside of marriage. She loves Rochester passionately, as is evidenced by their long kiss under the chestnut tree. But Jane has also been warned about the effects of passion unrestrained by reason—she has seen Bertha Mason.

Bertha Mason, the wife Rochester has imprisoned in his attic, is the incarnation of unbridled passion breaking out in fire and blood. Just as John Reed's unrestrained passion for gambling led to his suicide and his mother's despair, Bertha Mason's appetites have turned her into a beast and also into a vampire sucking the blood from her brother's arm and the life from her husband's heart and soul. Bertha represents the animal side of the human being, and since she has never allowed her spiritual side to develop, she has even come to resemble a dangerous, wild animal, strong as well as savage. Rochester had been introduced to Bertha by his father and brother, but he was seduced by her vivacious beauty, animal sexuality, and feminine charms. Rochester's "senses were excited" (268) to the point where he imagined himself to be in love with a woman he didn't know. Because his passions overpowered his reason, Rochester wed a woman he had barely spoken to. Incapable of becoming more sensitive, virtuous, or intelligent, Bertha instead becomes more and more depraved. Insanity runs in her family, but her sexual and alcoholic excesses have contributed to her premature descent into savagery and madness. Her huge size symbolizes her gluttony for all worldly pleasures, including eating and drinking.

Rochester points out how Jane contrasts with the loud, insane, heavy, raving woman he keeps locked in his attic, but many critics see Bertha as Jane's alter ego or double. Bertha is Jane's passion, anger, and desperation personified. Literally, Bertha must die before Jane can marry Rochester; figuratively, the Bertha in Jane must die before Jane can be ready for marriage. Bertha's outrageous beastliness represents Jane's fear of an overwhelming sexuality; Bertha's imprisonment and rage represent the secret dread Jane has of marrying someone so much more powerful and wealthy than she is.

Besides resisting the temptation of passionate sexuality, Jane must also resist her desire to be totally absorbed into Rochester's will and personality. Even though she loves Rochester desperately, she realizes that succumbing to another's will without the power or the means to assert her own will is a sort of suicide. This same voice of Nature that has told Jane to flee temptation will also help her escape a similar fate as St. John River's wife. To maintain her integrity as a person, Jane realizes that she must be treated as an equal partner, not as a dependent or as a tool.

Her uncle's fortune allows Jane the financial independence she needs to find her proper sphere, and Rochester's reduced physical and social power allow Jane to safely marry him without fear of being completely extinguished. Critics like Pauline Nestor believe that Jane has only found the symbiotic pre-Oedipal relationship she has always desired—the relationship between a parent and an infant, in which two personalities are entirely merged. Others, like Adrienne Rich, see Jane progressing from an angry, desperate child who pleases others only to be loved to a woman of independent mind and spirit who has finally found the equal spiritual and mental union she has craved.

Jane has asserted her right to be valued as an individual and not just an appendage to a man, but the end seems to find her in a traditional marriage, at her husband's beck and call. Either she has decided to accept the values of the patriarchy now that she has found an acceptably high place within the social system (as critics like Jina Politi and Terry Eagleton claim) or her marriage is not quite the traditional one, since it is based more on love and suitable temperament than on status, money, or sexual attraction. Also, Rochester needs Jane much more than Jane needs Rochester, perhaps making their union more unconventional and "outside" patriarchal society.

Edward Fairfax de Rochester is the only other character who seems to change and develop during the course of the novel. Rochester has been an angry, resentful man, determined to snatch pleasure from life despite being tricked into a disastrous marriage with Bertha. Jane at first excites in him a long-dormant wish to be good, but not to do the right thing, as evidenced by his attempting to trick Jane into a bigamous marriage. After this plan is shattered, he urges Jane to become his mistress, even though his previous mistresses have all become contemptible to him simply because of the nature of their slavish dependence. After Jane runs away from Thornfield, all we know about Rochester is that he has attempted to save his insane wife after she set fire to Thornfield, although no one would have faulted him for allowing her to perish.

Left blind and maimed, Rochester is certainly a changed man. Where he had been rebellious, he now begins to "experience remorse, repentance" and "the wish for reconcilement to my Maker" (393). He understands his physical maiming as punishment for sin, and he sees Jane's arrival as providing the instrument of his salvation. In her presence his "heart swells with gratitude to the beneficent God of this earth" (393). St. John has gone to save his millions in India, but Jane has been called to save her one stray prodigal.

Jane, Rochester, and Bertha Mason are "hot" characters. Images of fire and heat surround them. In contrast, Mrs. Reed, Mr. Brocklehurst, and St. John Rivers are "cold" characters, who are always described as icy, hard, made of marble or stone. These cold characters do not change, because their hearts and souls are frozen or petrified. Mrs. Reed confesses her lie to Jane only to save her own soul; otherwise, she is as cold and unyielding on her deathbed as she was fifteen years earlier. St. John Rivers, also on his deathbed while writing the epistle that ends the novel, has never once wavered or admitted a doubt about the rightness and virtue of his every action. His heart might as well be made "of stone or metal" (362).

Miss Temple is also described as like marble, and her influence over Jane is very similar to that of St. John Rivers. "Miss Temple had always something of serenity in her air, of state in her mien, of refined propriety in her language, which precluded deviation into the ardent, the excited, the eager" (63), and St. John also prevents Jane from expressing her passionate nature. St. John "acquired a certain influence over me that took away my liberty of mind: his praise and notice were more restraining than his indifference" (350), but this could also be said of Miss Temple. Both characters have an unnatural, restraining effect on Jane's character. When Miss Temple marries and leaves Lowood, Jane realizes that "she had taken with her the serene atmosphere I had been breathing in her vicinity—and that now I was left in my natural element" (73). Similarly, Jane feels very much out of her natural element when with St. John Rivers: "I felt daily more and more that I must disown half my nature, stifle half my faculties, wrest my tastes from their original bent, force myself to the adoption of pursuits for which I had no natural vocation" (351). But with Rochester "there was no harassing restraint, no repressing of glee and vivacity . . . for with him I was at perfect ease, because I knew I suited him" (384). Jane's quest has been to find a human heart with which she can commune fully, holding nothing back, and Rochester supplies this need: "to talk to each other is but a more animated and an audible thinking" (397). The image of a conversation with another person being just like thinking out loud suggests that Jane has found the other half of her soul. It has even been suggested that not only Rochester, but all of the characters in the novel, are externalized representations of different portions of Jane's character, which she must either reject or accept.

What is remarkable about Charlotte Brontë's characterization is that while characters may be stereotyped, and even satirized, the satire is rarely humorous, because the narrative perspective does not allow us to distance ourselves from those being satirized. Brontë's contemporaries—including Jane Austen, William Makepeace Thackeray, and Charles Dickens—describe stereotypical characters from the point of view of a "superior" narrator who sees through their follies, stupidities, and evilness with a distancing humor. Charlotte Brontë's narrators do not feel morally superior to others: her protagonists are simply more aware of their own motivations than her other characters. This mode of characterization gives the novels a highly unusual moral and emotional intensity. Brontë created a new type of intensely interior characterization that is often more like Dostoevsky's than that of other nineteenth-century British novelists. Charlotte Brontë's greatest gift as a novelist may be this ability to understand and represent interior feelings and motivations, and her methods of characterization helped shape the subsequent history of the English novel.

THEMATIC ISSUES

In *Jane Eyre* we find many of the thematic issues that Brontë returns to again and again. The protagonist is an orphan who feels misplaced in the social order, misjudged, and mistreated. The social status markers of wealth and family have been denied her, so the heroine must prove her worth to the world in order to reach her appropriate place in society. Social class issues are complicated by gender issues, since women have so few opportunities for using their innate talents and expressing their true personalities. Women are confined to a limited sphere in life and are expected to be content with their lot, when in fact they are either going mad or dying inside. Religious dogma, almost always authored by men, also imprisons women in a far too narrow sphere. Religious zeal is just as oppressing as religious hypocrisy, when men use either to control women.

At Gateshead, Jane's physical, emotional, mental, and psychological confinement is emblematized by her imprisonment in the Red Room. The color red symbolizes her rage, and the history of the Red Room symbolizes the nature of her oppression. Mr. Reed, her uncle, died in the Red Room. Mr. Reed had been kind to adopt the orphan Jane, but as a *pater familias*, the first building block of a patriarchy, Mr. Reed represents everything that oppresses Jane as a female child. She is born destitute because her mother was disinherited for marrying a poor minister—but all women are at least symbolically disinherited in a patriarchal culture. She is tyrannized by her cousin John Reed, the inheritor of all that he sees. As a female, she has very few outlets for her abilities, talents, and desires. She can completely renounce the world and deny her self, as her cousin Eliza will do by becoming a nun and as Helen Burns will do through spiritual self-immolation; or she can spend her time and energies trying to catch a husband, as Georgiana and Blanche Ingram will do. She can starve herself to death, as she contemplates doing in the Red Room, or go mad, as she feels she may do in the Red Room. Even marriage does not enlarge a woman's options much, since Bertha Mason goes mad and Mrs. Reed, who thinks only to live through her son, dies in despair.

In a desperate bid for freedom, Jane makes herself so disagreeable that she is quickly sent to school, but the entire purpose of the school is to prepare poor girls for a life of deprivation, self-denial, and starvation. When Miss Temple leaves, Jane feels that she must have something more, even if it is only "a new servitude" (74), and leaves for Thornfield. But the life of a governess requires just as much self-denial, deprivation, and emotional starvation as that of a charity-school girl. Walking the battlements, Jane yearns for more of a life. Although Rochester appears to offer her marriage, he only offers her the life of a mistress, a Céline Varens, whose every thought must be on how to make her appearance and personality pleasing and fascinating to her man. Life at Marsh End soon becomes just as oppressive, as St. John attempts to crush her will and mold her into his helpmate. Jane's life as Rochester's wife at Ferndean can be seen as finally offering Jane the life of an equal partner.

As in all of Charlotte Brontë's novels, the protagonist is an orphan. While Brontë may have been attracted to this theme by her own mother's early death, most critics see the theme as either archetypal or feminist. Heroes and heroines tend to be orphans even in earlier fiction since their parentless status gives them more freedom, more responsibility, and a wider field of action. Mothers are considered to be a repressive influence on their daughters in a patriarchal culture, since, as critic Adrienne Rich points out, mothers are dependent and powerless themselves and can only teach their daughters how to survive by the same means: marriage to a financially secure male. The female child must be socialized and educated into complete submission, and good mother figures are therefore repressive, encouraging submission, while "bad" mother figures encourage rebellion and thus freedom. Jane can more easily rebel against Mrs. Reed as an "evil stepmother" than as a biological mother. Jane is thus mother-less for the very reason most fairy tale heroines are motherless: the wicked step-mother stands in for the mother, allowing the daughter to express her anger and resentment without as much guilt and fear.

Jane's status as an orphan gives her more freedom, and more incentive, to re-bel against conventional society than she would otherwise have, and rebellion against conventions is a central theme in the novel. Jane rebels against her un-just and unfair treatment under Mrs. Reed, even though conventional piety (and a few early critics of the novel) held that orphans should be profoundly grateful for any charity they receive. Mrs. Reed desires Jane to be "kept hum-ble" by her schooling, and Mr. Brocklehurst agrees, since "humility is a Chris-tian grace, and one peculiarly appropriate to the pupils of Lowood" (29). Jane realizes that the rich think humility is a virtue only the poor need to practice, and she is angered by their self-righteous hypocrisy, but the idea that rich and poor should be held to the same Christian standard was itself considered rebel-lious, if not revolutionary, to many nineteenth-century British readers. English society was very class-conscious, and the "great chain of being" idea that all per-sons were born into the social and economic position God intended them to occupy for the rest of their lives was far from dead. Rebellion against class pre-rogatives was rebellion against God as well as rebellion against queen and coun-try. However, Brontë is less interested in upward mobility through the class system than in the fate of those who are "misclassed," as she felt herself to be. Charlotte, like Jane, was poor, isolated, and unattractive, but on the other hand she was educated, intelligent, and highly gifted. Jane is in fact a lady, and in-sists, for example, that she is no beggar even when she has in fact been begging (301). She is being unjustly treated as a dependent, a servant, or an outcast, and the entire novel traces her struggle to find her "proper" social sphere as the wife of a landed gentleman. Her lack of beauty and money make the struggle more difficult, but her "inner" qualities of education, intelligence, sensitivity, and morality finally win her the place she deserves.

The only accepted way for a woman to achieve social status in Victorian Britain was a good marriage, and another important theme of the novel is the negative effects of such a social arrangement. Denied the education or oppor-tunity to pursue a career other than governess or teacher, and thus doomed to financial dependence or poverty and homelessness, middle-class women were discontent and "in silent revolt against their lot" (96). Jane suffers from "too rigid a restraint, too absolute a stagnation" (96) at Lowood and at Thornfield, but she resists the easy solution of becoming Rochester's mistress and dependent. Upon becoming engaged to Rochester for the first time, Jane also bristles at the thought of being completely dependent on him, forced to dress up like a doll and be a kept woman, albeit a married one. She tells Rochester that she intends to keep working as Adèle's governess and earning her salary even after they are married. Jane's desire for mental, spiritual, emotional, and financial equality with her husband is seen as rebellious and, by St. John, unchristian. Although Jane could have married St. John as his financial equal, he demanded her complete mental and spiritual submission to his life goals, a demand she refuses. She rebels against patriarchal religion itself by refusing the call to minister to others at the cost of her own life and spirit, but she does feel that God has called her to save one soul, Rochester's. She asserts that she has a right to follow her "call" as much as St. John does, and she believes the spirit that calls her is not outside of, but compatible with traditional Christianity.

Patriarchal oppression is directly tied to the theme of religious hypocrisy and self-righteousness. The rich, like Mr. Brocklehurst and Mrs. Reed, use religion to justify their oppression of the poor. Brocklehurst provides his pupils only the most plain garments to wear, in order that they be Christlike, yet his own wife and daughter wear silk dresses and curls and live in sumptuous extravagance, as if their very wealth would buy their salvation. Men use religion to justify the imposition of their worldview on women as well as on the poor. St. John is not portrayed as a saint but as a cold, hard, self-righteous, restless, pitiless, and ambitious man who consciously uses Christianity to satisfy his lust for honor and glory—to win these in heaven, if not also on earth. He recognizes that he has the heart of "a lover of renown, a luster after power" (318) and believes that as a missionary he can be renowned, powerful, and still a Christian, thus reconciling his "propensities and principles" (313). Are the Indians he goes to save as much to be pitied as Jane struggling against his despotic will? Jane recognizes that men and women consciously and unconsciously twist Christian principles to suit their personalities and desires. Jane simply allows herself to do exactly the same thing when she listens to the voice of the "Mighty Spirit" (370), but she does so with less hypocrisy or self-delusion. Her mission is to save her one lost sheep, and thus to save herself, because it is the propensity of her nature to do so, and principles must be reconciled with propensities. St. John's was "the ambition of the high master-spirit, which aims to fill a place in the first rank" (398), but surely, Brontë suggests, the little people have a place in the kingdom as well, even though in their humbleness they are not quite so sure of it.

While St. John Rivers is a hard, cold Christian who must impose his will on others, Helen Burns is a warm, soft Christian who accepts other people's injustice meekly. She "turns the other cheek," as Jesus counseled, and looks only for a heavenly reward. Jane cannot accept Helen's meekness, because, as she tells Helen, "If people were always kind and obedient to those who are cruel and unjust, the wicked people would have it all their own way; they would never feel afraid, and so they would never alter, but would grow worse and worse" (50). *Jane Eyre* was written when the rights of men and women were very much at issue in Europe and in America, and the legal position of European women was often compared to that of African slaves. As a child, Jane compares herself to a rebellious slave, with the slave's resolve to revolt or die. Although England had abolished the slave trade in 1807, many Englishmen still owned slaves in the colonies until 1833, when slavery was outlawed throughout the British Empire. Rochester owns or has owned a sugar plantation worked by slaves in the West Indies. Bertha, who as a Creole may have a mixed racial heritage, is Rochester's slave simply because she is his wife, and her imprisonment in the attic is only emblematic of her legal position. Like a slave, a married woman was "owned" by her husband under the law of coverture; her legal identity practically disappeared. Jane is frankly frightened to become Rochester's wife, because his legal power over her combined with his physical strength and unbroken will could easily have resulted in Jane's complete enslavement. Although no revolutionary, Charlotte was very much concerned with the need women as well as men have for sufficient freedom and opportunity to develop their inner potential. Unlike Helen, Jane refuses to accept "Christian" meekness or feminine docility as a reason to tolerate enslavement, abuse, or oppression.

HISTORICAL/SOCIAL-CULTURAL CONTEXTS

The nineteenth century saw the beginnings of the feminist movement in Europe. A married woman had few rights in England and no economic independence. She could not enter into a contract; she could not own her own property (unless it was specifically willed to her, in a complicated premarital agreement); any money she earned after marriage belonged to her husband; she could not testify in her own behalf, against her husband, in a court of law. She could not file for divorce, unless her husband's adultery was compounded by gross physical abuse, and divorce required an act of Parliament at an exorbitant cost, so it was almost impossible to obtain.

Although unmarried women had more legal rights, they had even fewer opportunities. While most middle-class boys received a classical education, most middle-class girls received a finishing school education, in which they learned such "accomplishments" as playing the piano or speaking French, which could help them attract a husband. They were not prepared for a profession because no professions were open to women. Most working women were household servants, farm laborers, or factory workers. The only "genteel" occupations for an unmarried woman were governess, schoolteacher, or companion to a wealthy woman, and none of these conferred middle-class status, but only some liminal status between servant and lady. The life of a governess was particularly unhappy and isolated because she was neither a servant nor part of the family; therefore, her only companions were the children, who usually knew that the governess was beneath them in status and had no real power over them. Jane is outraged that Diana and Mary are to return as governesses to "wealthy and haughty" families who regarded them as "only humble dependents."

The role of evangelicalism within the Church of England is also part of the historical context of *Jane Eyre*. Evangelicals stressed the importance of moral earnestness, a personal relationship with God, the reading of scripture, and active proselytizing. The evangelicals had managed to reinvigorate the Church of England by emphasizing faith and morality. During the reign of George IV—first as prince regent, then as king (1811–1830)—churchgoing had become only an expected social activity not intended to interfere with anyone's pleasures. The scandalously immoral lifestyles of the aristocracy, including the king, contributed to a cynicism about religion. For example, Lord Melbourne, whose married daughter-in-law Caroline Lamb was carrying on a highly public and scandalous affair with Lord Byron, said of the evangelicals, "Things are coming to a pretty pass when religion is allowed to invade private life" (cited Erickson 86).

Patrick Brontë was of the evangelical strain of Anglicanism, but he and Charlotte were also intellectuals who despised narrow-mindedness and fanaticism. Both Mr. Brocklehurst and St. John Rivers are also evangelical Anglican pastors, but they both exhibit the narrow-minded fanaticism that Charlotte rejected. Brocklehurst is determined to instill Christian humility in his students even if it kills them and is too unthinkingly self-righteous to notice his own hypocrisy at not living in such Christ-like poverty himself. The poor, he thinks, are to imitate Christ and show humility to the rich, who can pride themselves on their Christian charity. St. John Rivers is also fanatical and narrow-minded. Like Brocklehurst, he uses his religion to elevate himself, to satisfy his ambition, and he is also certain that God has revealed the truth to him and not to others. He tells Jane that God wants her to be a missionary's wife, but nineteenth-century Evangelical Protestantism held that each person, even female persons, could commune with God. Jane does not hear the voice of God confirming St. John's plan for her life. Instead, she hears Rochester's voice echoing from the wilderness and knows that she has been "called" as surely as has St. John. St. John tells her that if she refuses him "it is not me you deny, but God. Through my means" (360). But Jane, like a true Protestant, refuses to allow a mediator between herself and her God. She insists that her salvation must satisfy both her yearning for spiritual union with a human being and her moral standards. For Jane, God has an existence that transcends the New Testament as interpreted by males. God also created Nature, and the world, which St. John despises and rejects. Her God speaks to her once more through the spirit of Mother Nature, an idea Brontë adopts from the Romantic poets, especially Wordsworth. Brontë insists on her right to interpret the scriptures and religious dogma according to her own conscience, and she accords Jane Eyre this same right. In her preface to the second edition of *Jane Eyre* (1848), Brontë wrote, "Conventionality is not morality. Self-righteousness is not religion . . . appearance should not be mistaken for truth; narrow human doctrines, that only tend to elevate and magnify a few, should not be substituted for the world-redeeming creed of Christ."

Brontë was also a true believer in the Victorian pseudoscience of phrenology. Phrenologists believed that the brain was divided into many discrete parts or "organs," each of which controlled some intellectual or moral tendency, such as benevolence, selfishness, pride, or reverence. Since each of these organs was larger or smaller in each person, phrenologists held that the shape of the skull indicated the relative size of each of these organs. Thus personality, character traits, and intellectual tendencies could be predicted based on a careful examination of the shape of the skull. A "bump" of ideality, for example, would predict that the organ of ideality was larger in a person with such a bump on his skull, and that therefore that person was more idealistic than average. Jane and other characters seem to be able to read the interior character of a person by examining their exterior features, especially the shape of the head and face. Some critics suggest that Charlotte makes use of phrenology to justify a first-person narrator's quick apprehension of another character's interior motivations and character. However, her belief in phrenology as a science was probably more responsible for its appearance in every one of her novels.

LITERARY DEVICES AND CRAFT

Jane Eyre makes extended use of symbolism almost to the point of allegory. The names of places are symbolic, as many critics have suggested. Feminist critics Gilbert and Gubar point out that Gateshead is the "head" or beginning of Jane's journey, the "gate" she must pass through to begin her growth into selfhood. "Lowood" is not only a "low" point in her journey, but it is also a "wood" where the big bad wolf Mr. Brocklehurst takes her. "Thornfield" is where Jane will sacrifice herself, like Christ, with a crown of thorns, rather than trade worldly pleasures and comforts for her integrity. "Marsh End" should be the "end" of her journey because it offers her a life of integrity and only integrity, but at the same time it is a "marsh," reminding us of the Slough of Despond that Pilgrim encounters in Bunyan's *Pilgrim's Progress*. Jane is despondent, thinking how she will be sacrificing "half her nature" to marry St. John, and Mother Nature calls her back to Rochester. Jane finally settles at "Ferndean," an isolated cottage deep in the woods, the only place a true love can survive in Jane's world, with her wolf Rochester, now declawed and domesticated.

Names are also symbolic. "Jane" recalls the saying "plain Jane" and "Eyre" brings forth associations with "err," "heir," and "ire" or anger. Some critics feel that Jane "errs" throughout most of the novel and that Brontë is not very sympathetic with her errors. Other critics emphasize Jane's "ire," or anger and rebelliousness, as positive rather than negative traits. Helen Burns burns within, because she denies the importance of her earthly desires so completely that they are forced to consume themselves, and her, in an inward fire. "Edward Fairfax de Rochester" suggests the dissolute seventeenth-century John Wilmot, Earl of Rochester, poet, cynic, and profligate, one of whose mistresses was a famous actress, and who was known to disguise himself to seduce women. The names Diana and Mary may symbolize the virgin goddess of the hunt Diana and the Virgin Mother, both powerful female deities. St. John Rivers's name recalls the apostle John, whose gospel depicts a Jesus far more divine than human. It also recalls St. John, the author of Revelations, which Rivers often quotes; and even St. John the Baptist, whose denial of the flesh is seen in critical theory as a denial of the female principal, the "flesh," as opposed to the masculine "spirit," which transcends the flesh. To be "born again" means to deny the significance of the first birth, from the mother, and to embrace the second, strictly spiritual birth, from the father. Rivers is like Helen Burns in his complete denial of the flesh and the world in favor of the spirit and the world to come. Only Helen lives passively, "in calm, looking to the end" (51), while Rivers abhors "selfish calm" (344) and paces the earth passionately yearning for that future glory.

Characters also have symbolic physical characteristics. Both Brocklehurst and St. John Rivers are described as cold, hard pillars, as phallic symbols of a patriarchal culture. Miss Temple's marble pallor and stately posture symbolize her repression of all anger and resentment. Mr. Rochester's dark, thick eyebrows, shaggy hair, and muscular build symbolize his earthly manliness as opposed to the moral, social, religious self-righteous superiority of Brocklehurst and Rivers. Events and objects are also highly symbolic. The old chestnut tree that is cloven in half by lightning the same night that Jane accepts Rochester's first offer of marriage must be highly symbolic, since it is referred to several times. The tree, whose "cloven halves were not broken from each other, for the firm base and strong roots kept them unsundered below; though community of vitality was destroyed—the sap could flow no more" (243) could symbolize

Rochester's marriage to Bertha, which is dead except for the roots, the legal tie of marriage, which keeps them together still. It could also symbolize the coming split between Rochester and Jane, and their long separation, throughout which they have no communication but are still joined by the roots of their spiritual communion, their great compatibility and love. The blind and crippled Rochester refers to himself as the blighted tree, and Jane assures him that he will bloom again.

The plot is structured as a journey from one place to the next, recalling Bunyan's *Pilgrim's Progress* and every epic, novel, story, and fairy tale of self-discovery in which the hero journeys to discover his true identity. The journey of discovery and maturation is a highly mythic or archetypal narrative structure, and *Jane Eyre* is a powerful novel in part because of its mythic and archetypal elements (see Chapter 3). These mythic elements are the same elements that we see in fairy and folk tales: the orphan, the evil stepmother, the unjustly persecuted heroine, the evil stepsisters (cousins, in this case), the journey as quest or initiation, the scapegoat and sacrificial victim (Helen Burns), the initiation to adulthood by painful trial and ordeal, the discovery of one's true parentage or family, and marriage as the happy ending.

Opposing pairs of characters are another structural device. Rochester the overpowering sensualist and materialist is opposed to St. John Rivers the overpowering anti-sensualist and antimaterialist; the two evil cousins, Eliza and Georgiana, are opposed to the two good cousins, Mary and Diana. Working out the relationship between the pairs of opposites is an interesting critical adventure. For example, while Rochester and Rivers seem to be opposites, they have similarities also, since both want to completely overpower Jane with their will, subdue her spirit, and possess her mind, soul, and body. Important female characters—such as Helen Burns, Miss Temple, and Bertha Mason—can be seen as either exemplars of what Jane must avoid if she is to do justice to both sides of her nature or as symbolizing parts of Jane's character that she must subdue or shed in her quest for selfhood. Completely disowning her flesh would result in an internal self-immolation such as Helen Burns exemplifies. Miss Temple's departure from Lowood signals the end of that path. Completely denying her moral and spiritual side would result in the type of outward fire that consumes others as well as the self, exemplified by Bertha Mason. Bertha Mason's death signals the end of that possibility, although Jane had rejected it a year earlier.

Allusion is also an important literary device. Most allusions are to the Bible, while some are to *Pilgrim's Progress* or Milton's *Paradise Lost*. Allusions to Milton's Garden of Eden with its serpent abound in the orchard scenes surrounding the first proposal of marriage. The allusion to Matthew 5:29, when Jane compares leaving Rochester with plucking out her right eye and cutting off her right hand (261), is repeated when Rochester himself has his eye plucked out and his hand cut off to symbolize the radical nature of his moral reformation.

Point of view in the novel is interesting as well. The first-person narrator is ostensibly the mature Jane Fairfax Rochester, married ten years and with at least one child. A first-person narrator allows the reader to see everything and everyone from only Jane's point of view, but we see events from both the child and adolescent Jane's point of view and also, occasionally, from the mature, married Jane's point of view. Very seldom is there a "distancing" of the child's point of view, but there are enough such distancings to make us wonder about the attitude of the narrator to her former self. Does she pity the child in the Red Room, or disapprove of her fiery temper and uncontrolled emotions? Does the narrator sympathize with or disapprove of her younger self's revolt against an oppressive, patriarchal social system?

Almost every other event and object can be interpreted as symbolizing something, and the reader should pay careful attention to every event and object that is described in detail. For example, Jane's experience in the Red Room is not only described in detail but also recalled at later points in the novel. Being locked in the Red Room can symbolize being locked into a womblike space from which she must be born; being locked into her own ineffectual anger and desperation, which she must learn to control; or being locked into an impossibly oppressive patriarchal and hierarchical social system that will not allow her to become a human being and that she will do battle with for the rest of the novel.

ALTERNATIVE PERSPECTIVE: FEMINIST CRITICISM

Feminist criticism is a broad term that describes several different fields of study concerned with female authors and characters. One type of feminist criticism examines female characters in fiction by men and women to see how representations of women are affected by the dominant ideology of a time period, and how representations of women in fiction can actually effect social change. Another type of feminist criticism seeks to recover previously forgotten fictional texts by women in an attempt to construct a feminine literary heritage in contrast to the primarily masculine literary heritage taught in school. Feminist criticism may be primarily theoretical or primarily political or sociological in purpose.

Even Charlotte's earliest readers discerned a concern with "the woman question" in her novels, and feminist critics have long been attracted to *Jane Eyre* as a prototypical feminist text. Feminist critics like Adrienne Rich and Sandra Gilbert tend to see Jane's progress as symbolizing the journey all women must make through patriarchy. All women are born orphans, because they can inherit nothing except a legacy of submission and dependence. All women eventually realize their inferior position and become enraged by this unjust state of affairs, just as Jane becomes enraged at Gateshead. But the powerful forces of patriarchy will quickly crush this nascent spirit of rebellion—Jane is locked in the Red Room to remind her that she is completely powerless and at the mercy of others. A girl's only options, Gilbert and Gubar point out, are to run away, to starve herself to death, or to go mad, and these three methods of escape, which Jane contemplates in the Red Room, are constantly recurring themes in fiction by women in many places and times. Bertha Mason emblemizes Jane's rage; it is Bertha whom Jane must "kill" before she can marry Rochester.

Another trial most women must face, and which Jane faces at Lowood and again at Marsh End, is patriarchal religion. Christianity itself, following Judaism, is a "male-centered" religion, with a male god who decrees women's subordination to men. In *Jane Eyre*, men like Brocklehurst and St. John Rivers are completely sure that they speak for God, while women like Miss Temple and Jane are merely to listen to God's voice spoken through Brocklehurst, St. John, or some other self-righteous man. Helen Burns rejects the Calvinism of Brocklehurst and St. John, with its emphasis on damnation and the terrors of hell, and embraces a Christianity of universal salvation. Nevertheless she too easily accepts others' unfair judgments about her and feels that struggling against injustice in this life is not worth the effort, since all wrongs will be righted after death. Jane refuses to blind herself to hypocrisy or to accept another's judgments or vision of salvation as her own. She insists that she has the right to judge her own actions and that she herself has been called, not through St. John but through Nature, to her God-appointed destiny.

At Thornfield and again at Marsh End Jane faces another challenge many women face: how to resist being sucked into the vortex of a too-powerful male will, being made into a satellite and a tool, a dependent without a will or a self of one's own. Nature tells her to "resist temptation," not only the temptation to succumb to passion but also the temptation to give up the battle for selfhood by allowing another person, a man, to completely control her destiny. Jane finally realizes the feminist ideal of an equal union with Rochester shorn of his patriarchal mansion, his brute strength, and his "vision" for her life: she will now "see" for him and not vice versa. *Jane Eyre* is thus the archetypal Cinderella story with a feminist twist. Jane's similarities to Cinderella are unmistakable, but unlike Cinderella, Jane does not passively wait to be swept off her feet; she insists on and obtains a marriage of equals.

The plot of *Jane Eyre* resembles that of several fairy tales, which are often structured around universal dramas of sexual maturation. Critic Jean Wyatt describes how the relationship between the poor, dependent Jane Eyre and her rich, powerful employer can be seen as similar to that between a daughter and her father in a patriarchal nuclear family. Rochester alternately seduces and pushes away the confused Jane, as a father who (usually unconsciously) flirts with his daughter and then makes himself unavailable. Bertha represents the obstacle: the big, bad, mad mother who threatens dire punishment, even death, for such a transgression. Rochester must be transformed from a father-figure into a husband-figure, by making him less powerful, and of course Bertha has to go.

Bertha Fairfax Rochester is the concern of several third-wave feminist critics and is even the subject of at least one novel, *Wide Sargasso Sea* by Jean Rhys. Third-wave feminists seek to include women of color, lesbians, and lower-class women in the feminist debate. They claim that traditional feminism has been concerned only with the rights of white middle-class women and has ignored women of other races, from other cultures, or from the lower economic classes. Charlotte Brontë is certainly a British chauvinist, in that she consistently depicts the British as the most superior culture on earth, and Bertha, while she may or may not be white, is certainly not British-born. Her status as "Creole" means that she, and her mother, were born in Jamaica. Jane seems to accept as fact that Bertha must be insane because she is unprincipled, and that she is unprincipled because she is not British, and that therefore she deserves to be locked up in the attic. Jane's ethnocentricity and tacit acceptance of colonialism (the ultimate patriarchal political system) is apparent because she fails to acknowledge that Rochester's wealth, and the wealth of the British empire, flows from its oppressed and enslaved colonies, or, emblematically, from Bertha. Jane also clings to the prerogatives of class. While she feels that it is degrading to be a poor dependent, or to be a governess, she does not feel that it is degrading for other women to be servants, nannies, *bons*, or housemaids, simply because they, unlike she, were born into the servant class and are not educated. In other words, Jane plays out her drama of the struggle for equality and personal integrity without considering how her freedom and independence will be won on the backs of the lower classes and oppressed races, half of which are women.

Feminist critics will continue to be attracted to *Jane Eyre* as one of the first and one of the best novels to deal with a young woman's difficult progress from childhood to adulthood within a patriarchal culture. The emotional intensity of the first-person narrative has mesmerized many generations of female readers. Each new generation will reinterpret the precise nature of Charlotte Brontë's feminism or lack thereof, as the definitions of feminism continue to change and multiply.

5

Shirley
(1849)

Shirley, Charlotte's second novel to be published, was well received by the public but less well received by the critics. It suffered in comparison to *Jane Eyre*, as do most second novels published after a hugely successful debut. The only novel Charlotte did not write in the first person, *Shirley* is her least autobiographical. It perhaps disappoints those readers who expect another intensely personal chronicle of one heroine's interior life, because it is much more than a romance. Shirley is also a historical novel, and, more specifically, a "condition of England" novel. These types of novels, best represented by Disraeli's *Sybil, or The Two Nations* (1845) and Elizabeth Gaskell's *Mary Barton* (1848), explore the devastating social upheaval brought on by England's rapid industrialization during the early nineteenth century. An ancient and revered agricultural way of life was vanishing. A proud peasantry and a well-to-do artisan class were being ground into a destitute, dispossessed working class. Charlotte Brontë chronicles the misery caused by unrestrained capitalism in a particular time period, the period of the Luddite riots.

Instead of focusing on a single female heroine, as do *Jane Eyre* and *Villette*, *Shirley* consists of several plots that mirror each other thematically. The most political of the plots concerns Robert Gérard Moore, a recently arrived mill owner who, close to financial ruin himself, seeks to import new machinery into his cloth mill that will result in even more suffering and unemployment among the desperate working classes. The second plot concerns an orphan, Caroline Helstone, who is living with her severe, misogynistic uncle, the Reverend

Helstone. She falls in love with her half cousin, Robert Gérard Moore, but marriage seems impossible, since she has no dowry and Robert must marry for money, if at all. The last plot involves Shirley herself, the title character although we only meet her one-third of the way through the novel. Shirley's presence in the neighborhood as the very young, very single, and very headstrong mistress of an estate creates a disequilibrium in the social atmosphere that can only be settled when she marries—if only she would.

Shirley lacks the consistency in tone found in *Jane Eyre*, varying as it does from social satire to deep pathos. Charlotte began the novel in great hope for the future. After all, she and her two remaining sisters had just published very successful novels. Their literary future seemed bright, and the possibility of making a living as authors rather than as governesses was delicious. Before *Shirley* was half finished, Branwell was dead. Emily died less than three months later, and in another five months, Anne was also dead. Charlotte had battled desperately to save her sisters and worked ceaselessly ministering to them, only to find herself entirely alone with her aged father, the last surviving child of the Brontë brood. She continued to write *Shirley* only to save her own sanity. Shirley Keeldar became a commemoration of Emily's wild and free spirit, and Caroline Helstone became a commemoration of Anne's quiet faithfulness. Many later passages in the book resonate with the author's too-intimate acquaintance with the deathbed of loved ones, of the desperate hope that is, in the novel at least, saved from the pit of desperate despair only in the nick of time.

PLOT DEVELOPMENT

Shirley opens with the antics of three curates, young clergymen from three nearby parishes. They play minor roles in the novel but, because they were "scarce" in 1811–1812, the years covered by the novel, they enjoy a rather useless, dissipated life of social visits with each other. The setting of the novel is Briarfield, a small parish in Yorkshire, in the north of England. The law of supply and demand has been working for the benefit of curates, but against unmarried women like Caroline Helstone and against the cloth manufacturing industry. Caroline Helstone is currently undervalued, because the marriage market is overstocked. Like the cloth that sits unsold in Robert Gérard Moore's warehouse, Caroline sits "unsold" in her uncle's house, not because she is defective but simply because she has no dowry.

The Anglican Church is represented by Mr. Helstone, Caroline's uncle, as well as by the three curates. Helstone, Rector of Briarfield, is a hard, cold man who missed his calling as a military officer. The three curates are proud, silly, ineffectual, and one is a drunkard. Immediately contrasted to these representatives of the established church, which is in need of reform, are those who would destroy rather than reform it—the Antinomians, the Jacobins, the levelers, the Methodists, the dissenters of every persuasion. Mike Hartly, the insane Antinomian weaver who will later try to assassinate Robert Gérard Moore, and Moses Barraclough, the rabble-rousing alcoholic Methodist preacher, do not offer an acceptable alternative. Tensions between the dissenters and the Tories (supporters of church and state) first come to a head when Mr. Helstone, Mr. Donne, and Robert Gérard Moore await an attack upon the mill house by Luddite rioters. Instead of being attacked at the mill, they are summoned to a valley where Robert finds his new machinery destroyed and his workmen hog-tied in a ditch.

Moore is an enemy of the local working class not only because he is seeking to import machinery into the wool manufacturing business but also because he is a foreigner, recently arrived from Antwerp, Belgium, and therefore associated with the French and Napoleon Bonaparte. Moore, however, cares nothing for politics except insofar as it directly affects his trade. He wants the war to end— honorably or dishonorably—because if the Orders in Council continue to prevent trade with America he will go bankrupt. Even though he is attracted to his half cousin Caroline Helstone, he thinks it would be foolish to marry until he can support a wife. Instead of pursuing romance, Robert relentlessly pursues those who organized an attack on his mill (Moses Barraclough is eventually convicted and transported for organizing the raid). Robert warns Lina, his nickname for Caroline, not to think of him romantically because his only goals in life are to pay off his father's debts and to make his fortune.

When Caroline comes to understand that Robert will never be her husband simply because she had no dowry, she wonders how she is to endure the rest of her life surrounded by men who don't allow themselves to feel empathy, pity, or love. Her lot is made harder to bear after Helstone and Moore quarrel over politics, and she is forbidden to visit Robert and his sister Hortense. Caroline had been reckoning "securely on the duties and affections of a wife and mother" to occupy her existence (190), but now she sees only the life of an old maid before her. She would never consent to marry one of the curates, but she can't bear the thought of giving her entire life away through the selfless good works and charity expected of unmarried women. Death seems like an escape from a dreary, meaningless life, and Caroline sinks little by little into a deep depression, despite her new friendship with Shirley Keeldar.

Shirley Keeldar, finally introduced in Chapter 11, is an orphan like Caroline, but she is rich, young, and beautiful. From this point the romantic plot heightens in intensity. Hiram Yorke, a member of the landed gentry who had been one of Shirley's guardians until her coming of age, has already suggested that Robert Moore try to win the hand of Shirley Keeldar, for the sake of her wealth. Caroline is convinced that Shirley is attracted to Robert and that he will marry her. Caroline loves both Shirley and Robert and will not begrudge them their happiness, but her suffering is so intense that she asks her uncle if she can become a governess in order to escape the neighborhood and her misery.

Mrs. Pryor, Shirley's former governess and now her companion, warns Caroline that the life of a governess is miserable and that hoping for a romantic marriage is unwise. Mrs. Pryor has been unhappily employed as a governess and was unhappily married. She sees Caroline's despair and tries to help her, even offering Caroline a home with her when she leaves Fieldhead, as she will when Shirley marries. But while visiting Robert and Hortense, Caroline hears from Robert's own lips that he favors Shirley, and Caroline returns home and sickens with a fever.

Realizing that Caroline has lost the will to live, Mrs. Pryor moves to the rectory to nurse her. Desperate to restore Caroline's desire for life, Mrs. Pryor finally reveals the secret of her identity: she is Caroline's mother, the mother who ran away from her drunken, abusive husband and never returned to claim her daughter even after her husband's death. Mrs. Pryor had thought that Caroline's outward beauty and aristocratic features signified an inner corruption, as it had in James Helstone, her husband. But Caroline's spirit is like her mother's, and finally receiving the unconditional love she has longed for, Caroline begins to recover.

The focus of the plot now shifts to Shirley and Louis Moore, who is Robert's brother and tutor to Henry Sympson, Shirley's cousin. While Shirley lived with the Sympsons, after her parents' deaths, Louis had been her tutor also. The Sympsons are visiting Fieldhead with the express purpose of seeing Shirley safely married, and preferably not to Robert Gérard Moore, whom Mr. Sympson sees as a destitute foreigner. Shirley rejects several socially acceptable suitors, such as Samuel Fawthrop Wynne and Sir Philip Nunnely, because she is resolved to marry for love and only love, and Shirley is in the rare position of being able to "do just as I please" when it comes to marriage (512), as long as she has the will to resist her uncle's browbeating.

We learn that Louis has been secretly in love with Shirley for years, but now that Shirley is no longer a schoolgirl but a proud young heiress, Louis despairs more than ever of gaining her love, much less her hand, since he is a penniless tutor, one of a despised class of hangers-on like governesses. But Louis has a power over Shirley which no one else has. She confesses to him alone that she has been bitten by a mad dog and expects to die. Her confession lifts her spirits; she allows him to convince her that the dog was not rabid, only mistreated. Louis realizes that Shirley loves him as much as he loves her, but between them stands the gulf of wealth, position, and convention. Shirley would never degrade herself by asking a man to marry her, and Louis is held back by his poverty and pride. Finally he summons the courage to propose, and this courage is exactly what Shirley has required of him—he must have the strength to master not only her, but her money, her power, and her social position as well.

Robert finally returns to the district, after traveling the country and seeing the misery caused by laissez-faire trade practices. He confesses to Hiram Yorke that he proposed marriage to Shirley only to save his mill, but Shirley had rejected him with the outrage of a betrayed friend. A moment after confessing to Hiram Yorke, Robert is shot by an unknown assailant, in revenge for his having prosecuted the organizers of the attack upon his mill.

Robert lies near death at Hiram Yorke's house for several months. As Caroline had, Robert now faces a meaningless, lonely death, because he has rejected love and sentiment. Mrs. Yorke does not allow him any visitors, especially not Caroline Helstone, whom she thinks is harboring silly sentimental notions about her cousin Robert. Caroline finally manages to sneak in with the help of Mrs. Yorke's son, Martin. Robert, who had no idea why Caroline had never visited him, has tasted a little of the despair Caroline had previously felt. Robert hears how Mrs. Pryor had prevented Caroline's death through love alone, and realizes that Caroline can be to him what Mrs. Pryor is to Caroline.

Finally the Orders in Council are repealed, business booms, and Robert formally proposes to Caroline. A double wedding ends the novel: Caroline marries Robert Gérard Moore, and Shirley marries his brother Louis Moore.

CHARACTER DEVELOPMENT

Caroline Helstone is in many ways the protagonist of the novel, since we know so much more about her than about Shirley, and we are privy to her thoughts and emotions. Caroline is like a seed ready to sprout, but the soil in which she has been tossed is frozen, and the germ of her spirit is almost extinguished. Her mother has abandoned her, her father is dead, and she has been raised by an uncle who has no empathy for women or children. The only love she has ever known is that of her uncle's servants. The Reverend Helstone barely speaks to her. His own wife, who had died just a few years after her wedding, was rumored to have died of grief, caused by his coldness, contempt, and emotional abandonment. To Mr. Helstone, women are "inferior: toys to play with, to amuse a vacant hour and to be thrown away" (138).

Caroline's choices, as a young middle-class woman, are either to marry or become an old maid, keeping her uncle's house until he dies. The only "profession" open to women of her class is that of governess or teacher, and both are very poorly paid, degrading work. As the niece of the Reverend Helstone, she can expect to be propositioned by one of the curates, but they all repel her. She falls in love with her cousin Robert and begins to bloom when he seems to genuinely care for her. But when it becomes clear to her that Robert has no intention of marrying a penniless woman, whether or not he loves her, Caroline is crushed. She feels her life has no purpose, her abilities have no outlet, and she has no one to love or who loves her. The only relief from misery she can imagine is death, but she wonders, "What am I to do to fill the interval of time which spreads between me and the grave?" (190). Unmarried women are expected to devote themselves to charitable occupations, but Caroline's spirit needs more to sustain it. Soon after it becomes clear to her that Robert intends to propose to Shirley, Caroline catches a fever and, because she has no will to live, does not recover as expected but sinks closer and closer to death.

Mrs. Pryor realizes what is happening and, desperate to save her child's life, reveals her true identity to Caroline. For the first time in her life, Caroline feels she can give and receive unconditional love. She slowly recovers and finds joy in being her mother's companion, but her true potential for happiness is not realized until Robert makes it clear that he intends to marry her when business picks up. Caroline finally not only grows, but blooms. We see her confident, even playfully assertive, like Jane Eyre when she is sure of Rochester's affection and honorable intentions. All the love and tenderness in Caroline's heart will finally be utilized instead of wasted.

Caroline only recovers the will to live when she discovers one person—Mrs. Pryor—with whom she can share mutual, unconditional, and lifelong love. This kind of love depends on a stated relationship: mother-daughter, and later husband-wife. The love between friends may alter when one of them marries (Caroline knows that Shirley will marry eventually), but the love between relatives is, to Brontë, unalterable and eternal.

Shirley Keeldar, the title character, is not only young, beautiful, and wealthy, but she is also gifted with a sunny disposition, a wonderful imagination, and a free spirit. Without ever having married, Shirley is mistress of an estate (an almost unheard-of position for a woman), and enjoys playing the masculine role of business manager. She imagines herself an esquire, a lord of the manor, and the thought of losing her freedom by marrying is suffocating (223), unless it is to a man who is indisputably her superior in every way.

Shirley is directly contrasted to Caroline. Caroline's quiet despair acts as a foil to Shirley Keeldar's happy-go-lucky nature. A "foil" is literally the setting for a diamond or other jewel. The foil acts to bring out the beauty of the stone, and Shirley is a glittering diamond. Like Caroline, she is an orphan raised in her uncle's home, but Shirley never longs for or even seems to remember her dead parents, because the world itself is her home.

Shirley has no intention of losing her freedom by marrying for the sake of social convention. She is a strong-willed though not a masculine woman who tells Caroline she will marry only "a great, good handsome man" who is clearly her superior—her master. Most of Briarfield, and Caroline herself, believe that man will be Robert Moore, who, although not wealthy, is strong-willed, handsome, and considered the most eligible bachelor in Briarfield.

Like Emily Brontë, upon whom Shirley is modeled, Shirley takes tremendous joy in simply existing: "The fact of the world being around—and the heaven above her, seemed to yield her such fulness of happiness, that she did not need to lift a finger to increase the joy" (237). This joy results from a sunny disposition, perfect health, a secret love, and an unusually active imagination. Shirley's imagination allows her to soar above the cares of the world, while Caroline—"a poor, doomed mortal who asks, in ignorance and hopelessness, wherefore she was born" (239)—is weighed down with sorrows. While Caroline longs for her lost human mother, Shirley feels that her mother is "Eve, in these days called Nature" (316), the great creative, generative power that bore Titans, that contended with omnipotence, and whose spirit still creates a glorious beauty everywhere for those gifted with a receptive imagination.

But Shirley's Eve also has a human side; she longs to be claimed by a power greater than she is, as her French composition "The First Blue-Stocking" reveals. The only man who can tame and curb her is the man who has secretly saved her French composition for years, Louis Moore, her former tutor. Louis is her only confidant, and the only one who can ease her fears when Shirley thinks she has been infected with rabies. Shirley would never be so unfeminine as to woo a husband, and Louis would never be so presumptuous as to propose to a wealthy aristocratic lady. However, as they recreate their former positions of docile pupil and forceful master, Shirley allows Louis to declare his love. Charlotte Brontë's ideal romantic marriage is a true meeting of minds that erases all differences of class, wealth, background, and position.

There is a note of sadness at the end, that such a beautiful and free wild creature must be tamed and caged into marriage, but allowing her to remain free and strong would have been beyond the bounds of Charlotte Brontë's ideals. As a woman, Shirley's true happiness is to be conquered and subdued into marriage, because she believes that "a great, good, handsome man is the first of created things," above all women (226). To men as a sex she owes no allegiance or subordination, but she longs to be tamed and controlled by a superior mind. Once she becomes engaged to Louis, she immediately and completely abdicates her power and responsibilities as a landowner and mistress of a manor house to her future husband and master (592), who will now make every decision.

The character who seems to change the most over the course of the narrative is Robert Gérard Moore. Not being a native of the parish (or even of the country), he has no empathy for the suffering he is causing by modernizing his cloth mill: "He did not sufficiently care when the new inventions threw the old work-people out of employ; he never asked himself where those to whom he no longer paid weekly wages found daily bread" (61). He believes that his own relative poverty prevents him from having the freedom to feel for others: "Poverty is necessarily selfish," he claims (99). He is attracted to Caroline but feels that love itself is a weakness, and marriage would be ruinous. Love and marriage are only for the comfortably rich and the desperately poor, who have nothing to lose by it. Images of sterility and inhumanity are numerous. Moore is married to his work; his love is his mill, and his children are his "grim, metal darlings—the machines" (371).

Robert, like Caroline, demonstrates the "separate spheres" of masculine and feminine employment. He, like Caroline, realizes that men and women think about different things, and that the things men think about are more important: money is more important than love. He realizes that he has "two natures; one for the world and business, and one for home and leisure" (258), but he will not allow his second nature to have a sphere of activity until his first, mercantile nature is fully satisfied with its position in the world. He represses his emotional life to the point where he proposes marriage to a woman he admires but does not love, for the sake of saving his mill.

When Shirley humiliates Robert by her outrage over his proposal of marriage, which she immediately realizes is only a proposal to save his mill, he leaves Briarfield for several months, ostensibly to find and prosecute those responsible for the attack on his mill. But he also takes the opportunity of his anonymity in manufacturing centers like Birmingham and London to investigate the true conditions of the working classes. For the first time, he feels empathy for their miserable plight and resolves to be just to his workers.

Before he can put his resolve into action, he is shot and grievously wounded by the crazy Antinomian weaver Michael Hartley. While lying near death for many weeks at Hiram Yorke's house, he, like Caroline, comes to know what it feels like to approach a meaningless death without the love and affection of a soul mate. When Caroline finally is allowed to visit him, and tells him how her newfound mother gave her the will to live, Robert realizes that he needs love as well as financial security. He learns to separate credit and commerce from affection and to distinguish between financial ruin and personal dishonor (554–555). Like Rochester, Robert suffers a grievous bodily injury, and his spiritual and moral regeneration is symbolized by his physical recuperation. Although he does not formally propose to Caroline until he can support a wife, he at least makes his intentions clear. Robert remains to the end of the novel a man of business—he still plans to turn the beautiful valley into a mill village, and cut down the trees for firewood—but he has allowed his second nature a life as well.

Robert Moore's brother Louis Moore has been a tutor to Shirley's crippled cousin for many years. He is a brilliant and imaginative man with the ability to live with only his own thoughts, but "his faculties seemed walled up in him" (430) because of his position within the wealthy household. Caroline feels that he is imprisoned by his occupation. He never laughs or smiles and seems completely content only with the animals and children who love and obey him, since with them "I feel like Adam's son; the heir of him to whom dominion was given over" (433). Animals and children know and love him despite his poor and dependent position, but his employer, Mr. Sykes, believes in maintaining class and rank distinctions. Louis is devalued as a person because of his economic and social position, but Shirley doesn't care about wealth and rank. As Shirley's husband, Louis has found the place in society that he deserves based on his intelligence and ability.

Shirley and Caroline both believe in the importance of romantic love, but the novel is full of minor characters who represent the contrasting view. Mrs. Pryor, also known as Agnes Helstone, warns Caroline that romantic love is an illusion, and that most marriages are unhappy. To most people Mrs. Pryor seems cold, repellant, uncommunicative, proud, and incapable of love. Life as a governess has destroyed her self-confidence, and marriage to an abusive alcoholic husband has made her wary of trusting others. Mrs. Pryor married James Helstone only to escape the misery of life as a governess, not because she loved him, so she is like the majority of women who marry for money and security. Caroline is dismayed at Mrs. Pryor's warnings, as they are just like her uncle's tirades against love and marriage, and similar to those of Mrs. Yorke.

Mrs. Yorke is completely unsentimental and not a believer in love and romance. Even when Caroline describes the love of a mother for her infant, Mrs. Yorke replies that Caroline is a little fool to be guided by her feelings and impulses, and harangues her mercilessly on her sentimentality. Caroline replies that her feelings were given by God to be used, not to be repressed (387). According to Mrs. Yorke, women were born only to be household drudges, and "solid satisfaction is only to be realized by doing one's duty" (385). Mrs. Yorke's own daughter Rose also rebels against this dreary philosophy. Rose swears to her mother that she will use her God-given talents instead of trading her very life for the security of marriage. Rose feels that the type of marriage Mrs. Yorke has and advocates is only a slow and torturous death. Rose will eventually emigrate to Australia, where women are not as confined by social custom.

Hiram Yorke is also incapable of believing in romantic love. He had been desperately in love with Mary Cave, the woman whom the Reverend Helstone married and neglected, but he knows that the passion he felt was only an illusion. Had Mary Cave returned his love, he confesses to Robert Moore, he would have left her. Hiram Yorke has many similarities to Yorke Hundsen in *The Professor*. He claims to be a democrat because he despises all those above him in wealth, rank, or social class, and is generous to those below him in social status only because they respect and look up to him. He lacks the ability to empathize with anyone, because he has no imagination, and without empathy and the ability to imagine how others feel, romantic love is impossible. Mr. Yorke thinks it is only sensible to marry for money, so he recommends that Robert Moore propose to Shirley in order to keep his mill afloat.

Like Hiram Yorke, Mr. Sympson, Shirley's uncle, thinks of marriage as having nothing to do with sentiments and feelings, and demands that Shirley marry someone of equal or better station and wealth. Shirley tells Sympson, "Your god, sir, is the World" (518) and that she walks by another creed. Shirley is disgusted by the way marriage for money and position results in loveless marriages, infidelity, hatred, deceit, unloved children, and many other vices and miseries.

On the other hand, the Sykes family, who have six daughters to marry off, would think nothing of marrying one of their young girls to the fifty-five-year-old Reverend Helstone, who loves to flirt with their most "credulous and frivolous" child, Hanna. Because Helstone has a nice house, a good income, and is rumored to have a good deal of savings, they would have delivered one of their own over to him without a scruple, even though everyone knows that he is a hard, cold man who ignored his first wife to death. The second Mrs. Helstone would, after the honeymoon, no doubt crawl through the rest of her days as "a sordid, trampled worm" (139), but her parents would feel no responsibility for what befell her after marriage.

Caroline's uncle, Mr. Matthewson Helstone, is only one of the male characters in the novel who show how dangerous it is to marry for security, money, or position. Helstone is a positive misogynist. Women to him are a different and inferior species, and marriage is "pure folly" (124) since men and women can have nothing in common. He thinks his niece Caroline should be perfectly content with sewing and cooking, because he is incapable of understanding a woman's need for anything other than the material necessities of life. Helstone loves to be gallant with the silly young girls who visit him with their mamas, because they reinforce his opinion that all women are idiots, but he is incapable of imagining a serious conversation with a woman.

Mr. Malone, the Irish curate, has similar ideas about women being an alien species. He intends to marry only for money and social status, because marrying for love is vulgar and weak. He agrees with Robert Moore that women are only an impediment to a serious man of business unless they advance one's position in the world. Mr. Malone at first tries to woo Caroline simply because he believes, falsely, that she will inherit a good bit of money. But once Shirley Keeldar moves into the neighborhood, Malone immediately drops his ridiculously awkward courting of Caroline to woo the much wealthier woman, without even the pretense that he had ever cared for the less wealthy Caroline. Mr.

Donne, a curate like Malone, is so conceited that he thinks women cannot help being in love with him. Like Malone, he despises everything in Yorkshire, especially the poor, and seriously thinks that Shirley would love to catch him as her husband. These two men think that just because they are men, they are infinitely desirable to all women and deserve nothing but homage and adoration. Because mothers like Mrs. Sykes constantly parade their marriageable daughters before any man who has a profession and an income, these curates think of themselves as precious commodities, and plan to sell themselves to the highest bidder on the marriage market.

THEMATIC ISSUES

One of the most important themes in *Shirley* is the role of women in middle-class society. While lower-class women have always worked—in the novel they work in Robert's mill, or as servants, or as farm laborers, milkmaids, and the like—middle-class women were not expected or allowed to perform such demeaning manual labor. The goal of every young middle-class woman was to catch a husband, as this was the most desirable and respectable means of support.

Mrs. Sykes's daughters accept, eagerly or reluctantly, their profession of husband hunting, accompanying their mother on numerous visits and entertaining numerous guests at home. Rose Yorke completely refuses to play the marriage game and is resolved to emigrate as soon as she is old enough to leave the country. Rose is modeled upon Charlotte Brontë's good friend Mary Taylor, who emphatically believed that women should earn their own living, and who did in fact emigrate to Australia and set up a profitable business. Caroline Helstone is a romantic. She wants to marry for love, not security, but nevertheless her only ambition is to marry and have children. When marriage, except as a loveless farce, seems impossible, Caroline longs for an occupation to take her mind off of her misery. She longs "to have something absorbing and compulsory to fill my head and hands, and to occupy my thoughts" (235), but her uncle will not let her apply for a post as governess.

Old maids, like skilled workers, are superfluous, or redundant, because the matrimonial market, like Robert Moore's warehouse, "is overstocked" (377). They are like the unemployed workers, because they cannot pursue their "trade," marriage and motherhood, and because society refuses to help them or even to acknowledge that their existence is unnecessarily miserable. Women in general, and especially unmarried women, need "a field in which their faculties may be exercised" (378), just as much as the unemployed weavers need work and wages. Caroline is typical of many unmarried girls whose only plan is "to wait and endure" (247).

A woman's position was made doubly hard by what feminist historians call "separate spheres" of life and employment for men and women. By the nineteenth century, middle-class men and women lived in entirely different worlds. Lower-class men and women worked together; upper-class men and women were idle together, since by definition upper-class men did not "work," except to oversee the management of their estates. Only in the middle classes were men and women completely separated, with men at work all day long and women at home. The theme of separate spheres is a constant thread throughout the novel, exemplified in the relationship between Caroline and Robert. Men can only think about trade and money, since only through trade and money can they support their wives and children. Women can only think of love and relationships, since courtship and marriage is the only trade or profession they have been trained for. Both Robert and Caroline understand that they live in completely different worlds, with completely different value systems. The businessman, in this age of laissez-faire economic policies, cannot afford pity or empathy for his workers, because the factory owner who abuses his workers the most, who cuts wages the most, makes the most profit and drives the others out of business.

This refusal to feel empathy is an important theme in its own right. Men are particularly subject to this vice: Robert Moore refuses to even consider what misery he is causing among his workers; the curates have no empathy for the poor and oppressed; and Mr. Helstone has so little ability to understand a woman's emotional life that he never perceives Caroline's decline. Mrs. Yorke despises the sentimental and disparages Caroline for being sensitive and ruled by her feelings (387), and Mr. Sympson reminds Shirley that marriage is "a matter of common sense and common prudence, not of sympathy and sentiment" (516). But Shirley will marry for love and only love, and Caroline would rather die of a broken heart than make a "practical" marriage. Mr. Yorke's idealistic political views are ineffectual because he lacks empathy, and without empathy there can be no justice. People like Yorke, Moore, and Helstone, who allow their heads to rule, never realizing how misguided their ideas or their ideals are, can never have the control over people and events that they imagine they should have, because they never perceive individuals, only classes or social and political groups.

Man is not a machine, and society is not a machine. This is another important theme of the novel. The nineteenth century was fascinated with the idea of the body, and of the body politic, as a mechanism that could be adjusted and tinkered with until it functioned properly. But this view ignores the feelings, the spirit, and the soul. Robert Moore had thought of himself as a machine, but when he feels that "the machinery of all my nature; the whole enginry of this human mill; the boiler, which I take to be the heart, is fit to burst" (496), he realizes that he must acknowledge his emotional nature as well.

Other important themes include the proper relationship between men and women, love and friendship between women, and the power of the imagination to make "a hell of heaven and a heaven of hell." The ideal of affectionate sisterhood is contrasted with the pain and torment of romantic love between men and women. Shirley imagines that she could have a perfect relationship with Caroline if only Robert Moore did not get in the way all the time. "He keeps intruding between you and me: without him we should be good friends; but that six feet of puppyhood makes a perpetually recurring eclipse of our friendship," Shirley tells Caroline (264). Caroline cannot help feeling jealous of Shirley, but she acknowledges that sisterhood is better than romantic love: "Love hurts us so, Shirley: it is so tormenting, so racking, and it burns away our strength with its flame; in affection is no pain and no strife, only sustenance and balm" (265). Shirley doesn't feel that women should spend all their time thinking about and hoping for romantic love and marriage. Yet Shirley will marry, and Caroline cannot imagine herself as Shirley's devoted friend should Shirley marry Robert. Caroline longs to leave the country rather than to completely annihilate herself.

It often seems that Caroline's imagination harms her state of mind. Her depression makes her every thought bleak and painful. Shirley has a powerful imagination that carries her away from the worries of the world, as, for example, when she imagines nature as her spiritual mother. Both types of imagination, however, are useful if one is to picture and experience another's world, be they the unemployed poor or the opposite sex. Shirley is the first in Briarfield to start a relief effort for the poor, and Caroline the first to explain to Robert how the workers feel about his policies.

HISTORICAL/SOCIAL-CULTURAL CONTEXTS

Set in the years 1811–1812, *Shirley* is partly concerned with the effects of England's war with Napoleon. Napoleon was attempting to starve the British into surrender by prohibiting all of Europe and all neutral powers from trading with England. Napoleon's "Continental System" prevented Britain from trading with the continent. Britain retaliated with the Orders in Council, blockading Europe from America (a neutral power), which led America to boycott England and which would eventually lead to the War of 1812. The English economy, which depended on the export of manufactured products, was brought perilously close to total collapse. While the rich got richer collecting ever rising rents, the middle-class manufacturers suffered loss of trade and the working class starved. Brontë shows how the tensions between the workers or "operatives" and their employers, between the radicals and the conservatives, and between the Methodists and the supporters of the established church affect the personal lives of her major characters.

The situation in France had been directly affecting almost all areas of life in England since 1789, when the French Revolution began with the storming of the Bastille. By 1793, the French king and queen had been executed by guillotine, along with thousands of other aristocrats and enemies of the people in what is known as "the Reign of Terror." In France, the proletariat was in power for the first time in the history of Europe, leading to a chaotic bloodbath in Paris and making the threat of a proletarian revolution in other monarchies, like England, very real. Not only were revolutionary ideas being circulated, but Napoleon Bonaparte was exporting the revolution to as many European countries as he could manage to conquer. All of Europe had been at war for more than twenty years. The British economy was almost at a standstill, and the antagonism between the working classes and the bourgeoisie was reaching a climax.

The French Revolution had immediately made the British government repress all freedoms for the working classes; trade unions and even meetings of workers were illegal, there was no minimum wage, no cap on the number of hours that could be worked in a day, no restrictions on child labor. Laissez-faire practices of the early industrial revolution allowed employers to use any means short of actual slavery to make a profit. In 1809, the government repealed the last protective labor legislation. Skilled artisans were pushed out by the introduction of machines that allowed employers to hire unskilled women and children at much lower wages.

Yorkshire, the setting for *Shirley*, was a manufacturing district, and the valley Brontë describes manufactured wool cloth. The shearing frame, which may be the type of "frame" Robert Moore is importing, was an invention that allowed unskilled women and children to finish a piece of woolen cloth, replacing the highly skilled "croppers." Rioting, burning of mills, and frame breaking across the north of England was the result. The Luddites were organized groups of workingmen who attacked those mills that imported shearing frames and other machinery that was displacing a whole generation of skilled workers. Brontë based Robert Moore's politics and the attack on his mill on a well-known historical incident.

The suffering afflicting the unemployed working classes is directly compared to the suffering of the unmarried—therefore "unemployed"—middle-class woman, through the character of Caroline Helstone, who, like Charlotte Brontë herself, was an educated, well-bred middle-class woman without the dowry to easily attract a husband. Charlotte turned to writing novels to keep from obsessing about her unhappy passion for M. Heger, and her second novel overtly turns to "the woman question," the question of what England was to do with its surplus of unmarried middle-class women. Women should be allowed to enter a profession or a trade (235) to use their talents and abilities. Enforced idleness is just as difficult for an unmarried woman as for an unemployed worker. Being a governess was an unpleasant, unrewarding job, as Mrs. Pryor tells Caroline. The governess was in the awkward position of being above the servants in status and below the family. She was expected to act like a servant to her employers and like a master to the servants. She was on duty during all waking hours, often kept busy with needlework or other menial tasks when her charges were away.

Becoming a factory worker was not an option, as female factory workers were paid so little that many were forced into prostitution to supplement their income. Marriage was the only respectable profession, and both men and women often viewed marriage as a practical business proposition having little to do with the sentiments. However, even a woman who married a "good" husband might be ignored and scorned to death, as the Reverend Helstone's wife had been, and a woman caught in an abusive and dangerous marriage, as Caroline's mother had been, had almost no options. Divorce was almost impossible to obtain in 1812, requiring an act of Parliament or an annulment by the church. Since wives were "covered" by their husbands in courts of law, wives separated from their husbands could hold no property of their own, could not sue their husbands, and could not even *petition* for child custody until Caroline Norton fought for and won that right in the Infant Custody Act of 1839. Before that time, children born in wedlock were indisputably the property of their fathers, and Caroline Helstone's mother had no choice but to abandon her daughter when she fled her husband, just so that she could hope to support herself, under an assumed identity, without being pursued. *The Tenant of Wildfell Hall*, Anne Brontë's second novel, is about a woman who runs away from an abusive, alcoholic husband, "stealing" their young son, and who attempts to start a new life under an assumed identity so that she can keep her son away from his father.

In *Shirley*, Brontë criticizes the common practice of marrying for position and financial security alone, because where there is no love between husband and wife, children grow up never learning how to love, and deceit becomes a way of life. Through the character of Shirley, Charlotte Brontë imagines how it would be if women were not forced to marry for financial security. Because Shirley is an only child and a daughter, her parents have given her a man's name (Shirley), and she has inherited an estate, Fieldhead and its surrounding vicinity, including the mill house that Robert Moore rents from her. Shirley Keeldar is thus in a very unusual position. At the age of twenty-one, she has become entirely her own mistress, with wealth and land to support her. Most women would never inherit an estate: if no sons were born into a family, the estate and its title would be inherited by a male relative. Most women would never be completely free of a male guardian—father, uncle, brother, or even nephew—to whom they must answer.

Charlotte Brontë is playing with the ideal of complete equality for women: Shirley acknowledges that "she holds a man's position" (213) and often calls herself Shirley Keeldar, Esquire, or Captain Keeldar. Because Shirley is wealthy and independent of male guardianship, she is free to marry whomever she pleases. But when Shirley marries, all of her property will automatically become her husband's property, so marriage itself involves a complete capitulation of power, even for a powerful woman. Shirley therefore refuses to marry anyone unless she loves that person as her master as well as her lover, unless she feels awe and a little fear as well as romantic love. She realizes that her husband will be her legal master, and he must therefore be master of her spirit, heart, and soul as well.

LITERARY DEVICES AND CRAFT

Shirley is Brontë's only novel that does not employ the first person narrator, and it is often criticized as lacking structural unity. Neither Shirley Keeldar nor Caroline Helstone is satisfying as central protagonist, for several reasons. The title character does not appear until one-third of the way through the novel. Even after she appears, we never really know what Shirley is thinking. We see her most often from Caroline Helstone's point of view, and then from Louis Moore's point of view. Shirley acts as a catalyst to the plot, and as a contrasting double for Caroline, but not as a central consciousness.

We are very much in Caroline's mind through large portions of the novel, but then her story disappears for long periods of time, most notably from Chapter 26 to Chapter 32, undermining the reader's assumption that this is Caroline's story. The critics Andrew and Judith Hook argue that because *Shirley* is a historical novel, the focus is on society itself, not on any one individual; the novel examines how social forces affect the lives of various characters. For example, the Orders in Council and the resulting economic hard times convince Robert to propose to Shirley instead of to Caroline; the lifting of the Orders in Council allows Robert to marry Caroline. However, the economic crisis barely affected the upper classes—in fact, many became more wealthy as a result of higher prices—and therefore has no discernable effect on Shirley and Louis's story.

Point of view is at times problematical. We are privy to the inner thoughts of many characters, but the suspense of the plot requires that we not know what Shirley and Mrs. Pryor are thinking. We don't know that Shirley loves Louis Moore, not Robert Moore, and we don't know that Mrs. Pryor is really Caroline's mother. We learn Louis Moore's inner thoughts, not only by being privy to his thoughts and soliloquies (472), but also through the awkward literary devise of reading his private journal.

The most powerful structural device, according to the critic Sally Shuttleworth, is the parallel between supply and demand in business and supply and demand in love and marriage. The novel starts with the curates, who are valued only because they are in short supply, at least when seen from a more distant historical perspective. Caroline is "redundant," because she cannot sell herself on the marriage market, just as Robert Moore cannot sell his warehouseful of cloth. As soon as the economy picks up, Caroline is married. The parallel between the unemployed worker and the unemployed old maid is powerfully drawn in Chapter 23.

Another literary device used to structure the novel is the central metaphor of man as a machine and society as a mechanism. Robert Moore denies his spiritual side in pursuit of material success and does everything possible to suppress the emotional and embrace the practical, the reasonable, the material. Images of sterility surround Moore when he defends "his grim, metal darlings—the machines" (371). When Shirley claims that he would immolate her on the altar of his Moloch (499), his god, his factory, which demands human sacrifice, Moore begins to break down, realizing how he has abandoned Caroline and love for money. Caroline has almost died from a lack of nothing but love and sympathy, and Robert acknowledges a similar feeling as he lies recuperating at the Yorkes'. Robert learns that love, sympathy, and self-respect are just as important as food and shelter, proving that man is more than a machine.

While metaphor is used to show the dehumanization of people, personification is used to humanize nature. Shirley's imagination personifies nature, showing that the imagination can perceive the world and its inhabitants in either spiritual or mechanistic terms. For Shirley, nature is the earth mother and Shirley a protected daughter. Shirley is peculiarly gifted with imagination, and imagination is essential for the empathy necessary for social change. Mr. Yorke lacks imagination, and therefore he lacks empathy. Robert Moore learns to empathize after his trips through working-class slums in London and Birmingham, but he still sees nature as simply raw material for his factories: "The copse shall be firewood ere five years elapse," he tells Caroline (597).

Doubles and pairs are also an important literary device. Shirley and her spiritual sister Caroline marry two blood brothers. Shirley is the strong, independent woman who contrasts with the economically dependent and reticent Caroline. Robert is the materialistic, ambitious, driven eldest son, while Louis is quiet, sensitive, intellectual, and unconcerned with material wealth.

Imagery also contributes to the theme of freedom versus bondage. Shirley is often compared to a wild animal or wild woodland nymph who must be tamed. When Louis gains the affection of and mastery over Shirley's dog Tartar, a "significant smile" (430) appears on his face because he knows he has the power to conquer an equally difficult animal, Tartar's owner. Like a wild beast, she is finally "fettered to a fixed day [for her wedding] . . . conquered by love, and bound with a vow" (592). Shirley loved her freedom, but also longed to be conquered and tamed. She tells her uncle that she will only marry a "man I shall feel it impossible not to love, and very possible to fear" (514). Shirley must be tamed using the very techniques used to tame animals. The word "master" is used with purposeful ambiguity and double entendre throughout the novel. On the one hand it means "tutor" or "teacher." But Shirley also uses it to mean "husband" in the sense that a husband must be the master of his wife. The proposal scene (577) brings this double entendre to its climax. Shirley is a wild animal who must be tamed by a master, for better and for worse.

ALTERNATIVE PERSPECTIVE: MARXIST CRITICISM

The nineteenth century saw the rapid rise of industrialism under laissez-faire policies that allowed employers to pay the lowest wage any worker would take. Unions, strikes, and organizations of the working classes were forbidden by law, leading to starvation wages, horrid living conditions, dangerous working conditions, sixteen- to eighteen-hour workdays followed by unexpected layoffs during which workers were not paid, and the exploitation of women and children in factories and mines. Karl Marx (1818–1883), a German philosopher and political thinker, observed the rapidly changing social conditions in Europe, but especially in England, and foresaw a revolution of the working classes. He predicted that employers, moved by the profit motive, would continue to lower wages until the workers, starving and without political voice, would take over the factories and rid themselves of the bourgeois capitalists who had exploited them. The workers would again own the "means of production"—the tools and equipment necessary for the production of goods. Profit (otherwise known as "capital") would no longer be the goal of production. Equitable distribution of goods and services would be the economic philosophy of the communistic state that would be established after the overthrow of capitalism.

For Karl Marx the economic methods of production within a society form the "base" from which everything else springs—including religion, art, literature, and consciousness itself. History itself is the product of economic systems. Since literature reflects society and history, literature must necessarily reflect the economic forces at work in that society. Even when literature is not about work, money, and production, it still reflects a certain ideology, or way of seeing the world, which is the product of the economic system. Most people are not aware that their ideology, or worldview, is the product of economic forces, since everyone within a social group holds the same worldview, produced by the same economic forces.

For Marx, ideology could be purposefully created through propaganda, or it could simply be the natural result of a system of production. Ideology created by the ruling classes in order to reinforce their control over the masses creates a "false consciousness" in those subject to it. The primary example of this type of propaganda for nineteenth-century Marxists was state-sponsored religion that promised rewards in the next life for suffering, privation, and obedience to authority in this life. In our day, Marxists point to the propaganda machines in Communist Russia and Nazi Germany, and to the ubiquitous mass media—television, radio, newspapers—that ceaselessly promote consumer culture in the United States. Even works of art and literature not directly sponsored by the state can still be consciously ideological since artists depend for their living on selling their works to those with the money to buy them.

Ideology, however, can also refer to the entire mind-set of a people, including the ruling classes, which means that it is out of the control of any group of individuals. All art, like all religion, arises naturally from the means of production, since consciousness itself is dependent on the economic base of any society. Different classes within a society, however, may have a slightly different perspective on their cultural ideology because of their positions within that society. Literature can therefore be seen as unconsciously reflecting certain worldviews that are the product of the basic economic structure of a society.

In addition, class struggle, revolution, and the condition of the working classes can be mimetically represented in literature or visual art. *Shirley* is about class struggle, and Brontë perceptively analyzes the situation much as Marx does. The workers no longer own the tools of their crafts, as they had when they were artisans or small shop owners. The "means of production," having become larger, more expensive, and more complex, are housed in factories and owned by men of means. The workers own nothing but their ability to work, which they must sell on the open market. Their "sole inheritance was labour, and [they] had lost that inheritance—[they] could not get work," Brontë writes, and their misery inevitably generated hatred for those responsible (62). While Marx analyzed the conditions in England during the early years of the industrial revolution and predicted an inevitable revolution of the proletariat, Brontë sought to prevent that revolution by counseling empathy for the working poor, fairness in trade practices, and mutual understanding between classes.

According to Marx, industrial capitalism, through the division of labor into ever smaller units of disconnected work, breeds "alienation" because workers on an assembly line, or at a shearing frame, never see the finished product and do not sell it themselves. Material goods become "commodities," articles that are valued not for their use but for their exchange value or price. Even people become commodities, valued only for their economic productivity and not for their individuality. "Reification" occurs when all aspects of human life, including people, ideas, and social relations, become things rather than experiences.

Caroline Helstone, as a middle-class woman, is alienated from the material world, because she has a very limited function within that world. She recognizes that the life of a factory worker or servant would be no more rewarding, but she longs to use her creative powers in a meaningful way. She and all women of her class have become commodities, valued on the marriage market not for what they can do but for their price relative to others on the market. Robert Moore treats his workers as economic units of production, and he evaluates his marriage prospects based on their economic usefulness.

Marxists believe that in most cases one cannot step outside of one's own class-consciousness. One's reality is limited not only by one's society but by one's position within that society. While Shirley Keeldar toys with the idea of a masculine identity and with remaining sole proprietress of her estate, all the forces of culture bear down upon her to persuade her to marry someone to whom she can relinquish her responsibilities. Caroline Helstone is even more tragically limited by her class-consciousness. Unlike Rose Yorke, she cannot even imagine leaving England. Within England, she believes her only options are to marry, to be a governess, or to stay an old maid in her uncle's house. Limited by her class-consciousness, Caroline longs for death as an escape. The repeal of the Orders in Council saves Robert's factory and allows him the luxury of a wife, but neither Caroline nor Robert can imagine life outside their respective positions within a capitalistic system.

Charlotte Brontë's analysis of the class struggle in England may have been limited by her own middle-class consciousness, as for example when she portrays the Luddites as misguided innocents led by unscrupulous rabble-rousers. The basic theme of *Shirley*, that class struggles can be overcome by love and empathy between individuals, can be seen as an example of false consciousness caused by Charlotte Brontë's conservative religious and political views. From a Marxist point of view, counseling love when what is needed is a revolution can only be seen as catering to the interests of those in power. However, Charlotte's concern with social injustices and the narrow-minded attitudes that foster such injustices do lend themselves to a Marxist interpretation, as does her depiction of characters whose fates are more determined by the social and political forces around them than by their own individual free will.

6

Villette
(1853)

After the deaths of Emily, Anne, and Branwell, Charlotte hurriedly finished *Shirley* and then sank into a deep depression. The subjects she chose for her last completed novel are loneliness, isolation, and despair. The optimistic belief that hard work will lead to success, evident in *The Professor*, is nowhere to be found. The fairy-tale-like endings of *Jane Eyre* and *Shirley* are likewise abandoned, replaced by a grimly stoical resolve to meet fate face to face, without imagination to soften the darkness of love lost. Relatively few things happen in this novel, but the few events are marked with an emotional intensity presaging modernist novels like Virginia Woolf's *To the Lighthouse* or James Joyce's *Ulysses*. The mind of the narrator, rather than the events of her life, is the true subject of *Villette*, just as it will be in the twentieth-century modernist novel.

PLOT DEVELOPMENT

Like *Jane Eyre*, *Villette* is a female bildungsroman, a novel that follows the development of the heroine from childhood to young adulthood. However, the structure of *Villette* is less like an ascent up a staircase than the cyclical ebb and flow of the tide. The sea plays a major metaphorical role in the novel, and the ebb and flow of hope is a major structural device.

We first meet Lucy Snowe as a fourteen-year-old staying with her godmother Mrs. Bretton in Bretton, England. A young child, Polly Home, soon comes to stay with Mrs. Bretton also, following the death of her mother. Polly is almost in despair at having been temporarily abandoned by her father, but she soon becomes quite attached to Mrs. Bretton's son, John Graham Bretton, a schoolboy two years older than Lucy. Lucy is a quiet, calm observer of the life around her. She enjoys staying at her godmother's because "one child in a household of grown people is usually made very much of" (61). Her icy coolness may be attributed to her unacknowledged jealousy that Polly has usurped the place of special visitor. Polly will return later in the novel to again usurp the place of special friend to Graham Bretton. Lucy is superseded by a more fortunate, more beautiful, more engaging child, and she withdraws even more deeply into her shell of icy reserve.

After six months with the Brettons, Lucy returns home, but of this home we hear nothing, except that she is not happy to be returning to this place of trouble. As a narrator, Lucy Snowe is infamously unforthcoming about some things, and one of those things is her immediate family. She says that the reader may imagine that she was happy for some years, as "the amiable conjecture does no harm" (94), and her comment that "a great many women and girls are supposed to pass their lives" in a sort of calm and peaceful daydream implies that she herself has not had the pleasure of such an easy, blissful life, even before the tragedy that leaves her alone in the world. The nature of the calamity is unspecified: perhaps some fatal illness carries off her entire family, as tuburculosis had carried off all of Charlotte's sisters. The metaphor of a shipwreck is used to allude to the tragedy, foreshadowing the shipwreck at the end of the novel that will once more wash away Lucy Snowe's tentative happiness. The nightmare of this first shipwreck is still experienced by the narrator, many years later, as a time when "we cast with our own hands the tackling out of the ship; a heavy tempest lay on us; all hope that we should be saved was taken away" (94). The image of the passengers casting everything overboard and praying to be saved, only to be lost, will haunt the entire novel. Hope has come to naught.

Left alone and without means, Lucy first becomes the attendant of an old crippled woman, Miss Marchmont, in whose house "two hot, close rooms" become her entire world. Lucy is buried alive, but she makes no move to escape, because she has been "disciplined by destiny" to demand nothing, to hope for nothing (97). The story Miss Marchmont tells the evening before her death, about her year of happiness followed by the death of her betrothed, foreshadows Lucy's brief happiness with M. Paul. Miss Marchmont also promises to remember Lucy in her will but dies before she has time to change it. The theme of a hope so close to fulfillment crushed in an instant will repeat itself again and again.

Just as Nature had spoken to Jane Eyre in her time of need, Nature sends Lucy Snowe, left desolate and homeless again after Miss Marchmont's death, the thought that she must "leave this wilderness and go out hence" (104). Lucy first travels alone to London, then takes a ship to Labassecour (Belgium), having heard that Englishwomen can easily find work there in a school or private home, tutoring children in English. Hope springs up again: forced to exert herself, Lucy finds that she likes the excitement of her journey. On board ship Lucy first meets the seventeen-year-old Ginevra Fanshawe, traveling to school on the continent; Ginevra informs Lucy that Madame Beck may be looking for an English governess for her children.

High spirits are followed by sickness on the crossing, and by fear and despair in Villette. After spending the night in a hotel, Lucy travels by coach to Villette (Brussels), the capital of Labassecour, only to find that her luggage has been left behind. An Englishman helps her negotiate for her luggage—that Englishman turns out to be a doctor who works for Madame Beck's establishment, and also Lucy's godmother's son, although they do not recognize each other. The Englishman walks Lucy through the park to a street with hotels, and this act of kindness to a stranger foreshadows the future relationship between the two. However, no sooner is she alone than Lucy is accosted by two drunken men on the street, loses her way, and ends up on the doorstep of Madame Beck's Pensionnat de Demoiselles (Ladies' Boarding School) in the Rue Fossette, and Providence whispers that this is the inn she had been seeking.

Even though Lucy cannot supply a single reference, Madame Beck hires Lucy as a child-nurse, after a phrenological assessment by M. Paul, because she feels Englishwomen are reliable and trustworthy. But when Madame Beck decides that Lucy must be an English teacher at the Rue Fossette, Lucy balks, since her French is limited and her ambition nonexistent. Only when she senses a direct challenge to her pride does she finally pick up the gauntlet thrown down by Madame Beck, enter the huge, boisterous class of foreign girls, and manage to command their respect and attention.

Lucy has been promoted, and she has learned that she can do a difficult job well, but she receives as little personal satisfaction from teaching as her spoiled, lazy pupils do from learning. She makes no friends among the teachers because she feels that they are not like her and can never truly know her. Even when Lucy recognizes the new doctor at the Rue Fossette as the man who assisted her upon her arrival in Villette, she does not speak to him. After close observation, Lucy is convinced that Dr. John is no other than her godmother's son, John Graham Bretton, but she does not reveal this to him because she was "not in the habit of speaking to him" (163). Because she is unobserved, Lucy can be very observant, and because she is rarely spoken to, she chooses not to speak. She is happy to remain unknown and unrecognized because "in quarters where we can never be rightly known, we take pleasure, I think, in being consummately ignored" (164). Even we the readers do not know her past, presumably because we, like all her new acquaintances, could not possibly understand or appreciate the tragedy of it. She has long given up the hope of ever being truly known and understood by another human being and therefore has little true desire to make friends or even to reveal her true nature.

The only person who seems to notice Lucy is M. Paul Emanuel, the literature professor who teaches at both the men's college and the girls' boarding school. When he is in need of a substitute actress for his skit, during Madame Beck's fête, he throws the part on Lucy and locks her in the attic until she has learned it. Lucy plays the part of a foppish man making love to a beauty played by Ginevra and is surprised to find that she likes acting and can act well. But after the play, Lucy vows never to allow herself such a pleasure again: "The strength and longing must be put by; and I put them by, and fastened them in with the lock of a resolution which neither Time nor Temptation has since picked" (211). Lucy feels that a woman without family, friends, or money cannot allow herself to be thus exposed to public view but must instead haunt the shadows and corners as a necessary defense against the world.

Lucy has long been sinking into despair. She can see nothing to hope for or to live for, because she is afraid to hope, to presume on good fortune when good fortune has never attended her in the past. During the long vacation, when everyone except one servant and a retarded pupil leaves the school, Lucy sinks into an almost psychotic depression. When she can sleep at all, it is only to experience such disturbing nightmares that death itself begins to look not like an escape from suffering but a doorway into even greater alienation and despair. The school becomes "a crushing tomb" and Lucy, buried alive, is most deeply oppressed by "that insufferable thought of being no more loved, no more owned" (232).

Almost delirious with despair, Lucy feels compelled to enter a Roman Catholic church and to confess to the priest, thinking that this step "could not make me more wretched" (233). The priest listens sympathetically to her confession, urges her to convert to Catholicism, and invites her to visit him at his home. As soon as a living human being reaches out to help her, however, Lucy retreats, afraid to lose her integrity under another's influence. She would no sooner have visited the priest than walked into "a Babylonish furnace," for fear of losing the core of her being (235). Leaving the church in a cold rain, she loses her way and faints on the street. Volume I ends with Lucy physically and metaphysically lost, alone, unable even to ask for help, lying near death on a foreign street.

Volume II will begin a sort of rebirth for Lucy, a second chance, after the death and descent into hell she has suffered during the long vacation at the Rue Fossette. Upon awakening at Mrs. Bretton's house on the outskirts of Villette, Lucy thinks she must be delusional because she recognizes many of the objects in the room as items from her past. She imagines her room as "like a cave in the sea," and the world as so far above her that "the rush of its largest waves, the dash of its fiercest breakers could sound down in this submarine home, only like murmurs and a lullaby" (225). This imagery suggests that Lucy is in a womblike environment, waiting to be reborn. Her godmother will be her second birthmother, and Dr. John will be the attending physician.

Lucy is grateful to find that she still has friends and hopes to be kept alive by occasional visits with them. She feels that it would be foolish to hope for too much from the Brettons, because they are not "well-matched and congenial" with her temperament, but a ray of hope does escape from her, if only because her need for friends is so great. She struggles to subdue her great need and longing, to expect what reason alone teaches her to expect, and to present a calm, cool face to the world.

For the first time, Lucy is shown around the sights of Villette. Finally living again, Lucy must decide how to live and what kinds of life are available to her. Besides the examples of Madame Beck and Ginevra Fanshawe, Lucy reflects on works of art, such as the Rubenesque portrait of the barely clothed Cleopatra and the work of art preferred by M. Paul, "The Life of a Woman," a series of four paintings depicting girlhood, marriage, motherhood, and widowhood. Lucy finds the Cleopatra repulsive in its fleshy laxity and coarseness, but "La vie d'une femme" is just as bad in a different way. Lucy rejects both the carnal and the demure representations of women by men. Later she will attend a performance by the great tragic actress Vashti, who has also rejected these role models for women, but Vashti's rebelliousness is also unacceptable to Lucy.

Lucy's weeks of pleasure are followed by despair when she returns to her boarding school. Her spirits are upheld only by Graham's promise to write. Reason warns Lucy to crush any hope she may have for this relationship, but when a letter does finally arrive, Lucy is delirious with joy. She escapes to the attic for privacy but is terrified to see a nun there, and she flies to Madame Beck for help. The gothic element of the plot is introduced with the appearance of the legendary medieval nun who was supposedly buried alive in the garden of the school, which was formerly a convent. Lucy also feels "buried alive" at Madame Beck's, and the nun's ghost is said to haunt the garden, which is Lucy's favorite retreat. The nun is yet another role model—the one Lucy has been the closest to embracing—representing re*nun*ciation and asceticism. But this role has already driven Lucy to the point of insanity once before. According to critic Janice Carlisle, the nun represents the refusal to desire, and "the sin in *Villette* is not desire, but the repression of desire" (282).

The expression of desire, however, can be equally deadly, as Lucy learns by watching Vashti act. Vashti, a woman the opposite of the languid, fleshy Cleopatra, is all spirit, but her strength is satanic, the strength to rebel until the bitter end. Lucy admires her strength but is quite horrified that Vashti has obviously passed through the burning fires of life without finding any peace, wisdom, or grace. Not only has Vashti not found peace, but men like Dr. John judge her as an indecorous woman, not as a great actress who has sold her soul for her art.

Vashti's performance does, however, reveal Dr. John's true character to Lucy. Dr. John cannot understand Vashti's mental suffering or the greatness of her art; he judges her as an unseemly woman, not an artist. When the theater catches on fire at the climax of the play, Dr. John leaps into the world of action, where he is at home, and rescues a young girl who has been trampled in the frenzy, a girl whose "refinement, delicacy, and perfect personal cultivation" contrasts with not only Vashti's but with Ginevra Fanshawe's bearing as well. This girl turns out to be the seventeen-year-old Polly Home, now Paulina Mary Home de Bassompierre, as her father has inherited a title.

Again superseded by Paulina Home, Lucy is forgotten in her prisonlike school while Dr. John is admitted as physician into the Bassompierre home. Lucy again begins to sink into despair, with "the sick dread of entire desertion" (349), not so much because she is in love with Dr. John but because she had begun to count on him as her only friend, her only correspondent, and her only ticket to the world outside the Rue Fossette. Lucy already realizes that Dr. John is not the perfect match for her, but she still hoped that their friendship could last.

Just as Lucy is about to go mad from "solitary confinement" (356) she is invited to the Brettons, where she again meets Paulina. Like Graham, the pampered, deeply loved, and protected Polly can never really understand Lucy, but she does like Lucy and invites her to spend time with the Bassompierres. Lucy notices the growing attraction between Polly and Graham and decides that Polly is worthy of Graham and vice versa. Bereft of hope for even his friendship, Lucy buries her love for John with his letters. Just as she finishes this task, she sees the nun for the second time. Lucy has again decided to kill desire, but the nun warns her that this path leads only to madness.

While John Bretton and Polly Home proceed with their courtship, Lucy and M. Paul proceed with their tortuous attempts to establish a closer relationship. M. Paul has been jealous of Lucy's interest in Dr. John, and he has angered Lucy with his coarse comments, as she has angered him by small acts of independence and rebellion. M. Paul has also seen the nun, as he has also buried his desire and renounced passion. Lucy and M. Paul both realize that they have much in common, but they are both afraid to take the risk of beginning a human relationship.

Just as Lucy begins to hope for true love, she is sternly warned to retreat during her visit to Madame Walravens, an ancient, hunchbacked, witchlike woman who lives in a strangely gothic dark old house. Lucy feels as if she is in a fairy tale, with witches, pictures that disappear, hunchbacks, a raging thunderstorm, and a strange tale of enthrallment. From Père Silas, Lucy learns M. Paul's history, but when she returns to the Rue Fossette she begins to suspect that her visit to Madame Walravens was plotted by Père Silas, Madame Beck, and Madame Walravens, in order to dissuade her from pursuing a relationship with M. Paul.

This time Lucy vows not to renounce desire. Soon M. Paul and Lucy declare their friendship for each other, a moment of unhoped-for happiness in Lucy's bleak and dreary life. But after this moment of happiness, M. Paul makes himself inexplicably unavailable to Lucy. Finding a Catholic tract in her desk, Lucy realizes that Père Silas has counseled Paul not to associate with a heretic, who is perhaps even an atheist, since Lucy attends churches of different denominations as the mood strikes her. But Lucy sees only "minute and unimportant differences" between the Lutheran, Episcopalian, and Presbyterian religions and tells Paul that only "the Bible itself, rather than any sect, of whatever name or nation" is her spiritual guide (514). Paul finally accepts that her faith is as sincere as his own, even though it is expressed differently.

While Lucy resists the temptation to change herself for M. Paul, Polly Home easily melds into the beloved and then wife of Graham Bretton. Polly's fortune is symbolized by her plaiting together locks of her, Graham's, and her father's hair, and imprisoning them in a locket. Lucy compares Graham and Paulina's fortune to that of "Jacob's favoured son" (533) and accepts stoically the fate God has assigned to her. Jacob's brothers were envious and cast him into a pit, but Lucy will not be actively envious. She accepts that God favors whom He will and that his ways are unfathomable to men. But she accepts this with despair, as she writes, "His will be done, as done it surely will be, whether we humble ourselves to resignation or not" (534). We do not choose to do His will, we rather accept what He wills for us, as there is no use complaining or rebelling.

No sooner do Lucy and M. Paul become close again than she is informed he must leave the country for several years. Madame Beck has prevented her from seeing M. Paul before his departure, and she even slips Lucy a strong dose of opium the evening of Paul's supposed departure. The opium has an unexpected effect: instead of sleeping, Lucy becomes more awake than she has ever been. Imagination is released from the bonds of reason; desire is loosed from the bonds of repression, social anxiety, and fear. Lucy rises, dresses, and sneaks out of the house, surprised at how easy it is to escape the prisonlike school.

Instead of deserted streets, Lucy finds that a celebration is taking place in Villette, and night has been turned into day. The opium seems to make Lucy hyper-aware; she has escaped the dungeon of her despair and entered into a throng of colorful festivity. In her opium-induced trancelike state, Lucy sees many people whom she knows without being observed by them, including Madame Beck, surrounded by Madame Walravens, Père Silas, and Paul

Emanuel himself, whom she thought never to see again. Observing the way M. Paul interacts with Justine Marie, his young, beautiful, and rich ward who is named after his once fiancée, long dead, Lucy assumes that he will marry her. Attempting to crucify herself on the cross of resignation and reason, she instead feels the vulture of jealousy tearing her entrails apart. She returns alone to the Rue Fossette, only to encounter the nun again, this time sleeping in her bed. Approaching the bed and observing no movement, Lucy discovers that this nun is only a nun's habit stuffed with pillows, bearing an anonymous message that the nun will be seen in the Rue Fossette no more.

Lucy has been totally unable to resign herself, to deny her desire and jealousy, and therefore the nun is killed, dismantled, shown to be a fraud. The next morning, Lucy is confirmed in her suspicion that Ginevra's lover de Hamal was the nun when it is discovered that Ginevra has disappeared. Eventually she receives a letter from Ginevra describing their elopement. The nun was a disguise used by de Hamal to gain access to Ginevra: the disguise of a celibate masked a most illicit and reckless passion. The nun still symbolizes Lucy, but it is now clear that her celibate exterior hides a seething cauldron of passion. The freedom and renovation she has attempted to gain by self-crucifixion have not materialized. "They [freedom and renovation] had boasted their strength loudly when they reclaimed me from love and its bondage, but upon my demanding deeds, not words, some evidence of better comfort, some experience of a relieved life—Freedom excused himself, as for the present, impoverished and disabled to assist; and Renovation never spoke; he had died in the night suddenly" (579). Again the hope of happiness recedes from the shore, only to return in the shape of M. Paul, promising to reveal a secret before his departure. He has set up a school for her, and in so doing he has once more brought happiness to Lucy's life. That happiness becomes complete when she learns that M. Paul is not going to marry his ward but would like to marry Lucy when he returns.

For the first time, Lucy sustains a hope of happiness for a lengthy period of time. For three years, "the three happiest years of my life," she waits for M. Paul's return, working hard because she has hope. "At parting, I had been left a legacy; such a thought for the present, such a hope for the future, such a motive for a persevering, a laborious, an enterprising, a patient and brave course" (594). But like all Lucy's hopes, this one is seemingly crushed also when a huge storm blows up at the time of M. Paul's voyage home and wrecks many ships on the Atlantic. Is M. Paul's ship wrecked as well? The naive reader is left free to imagine a happy ending, with faith, hard work, perseverance, and goodness of heart rewarded, but the realist is allowed to see that only the selfish and wicked prosper, with Madame Beck, Père Silas, and Madame Walravens living long and prosperous lives. The tide of hope has gone out, perhaps forever, for Lucy

Snowe, leaving her to write this narrative as a way to search for the peace of resignation.

CHARACTER DEVELOPMENT

Lucy Snowe is an enigmatic character, because she is unforthcoming, and perhaps unreliable, as narrator of her own life. We first meet her at the Brettons, where she claims to be unimaginative, unemotional, and calm. Yet the rest of the narrative shows that Lucy's imagination is her greatest enemy, that her emotional life is in constant turmoil, and that her icy calm is only a facade. After leaving the Brettons, she returns to a less than pleasant home situation, experiences an unnarratable tragedy that leaves her homeless and without family, and is forced to find a means of support. Lucy treats the reader much as she treats everyone she meets: she never reveals the tragedy and trauma of her past because it cannot be understood by anyone who has not experienced it. The reader of a novel must be of the same class as Mrs. Bretton, someone blessed with good fortune and a good disposition, to whom devastating tragedy is unknowable.

Lucy claims she is "inadventurous, unstirred by impulses of practical ambition" (139) but she may be so traumatized by past experiences that she is afraid to try her luck or challenge her fate in any way. However, she takes several daring and positive steps, such as traveling alone to London and then to Villette, while claiming that it was fate that drove her to these measures. Perhaps, as critic Brenda R. Silver claims, Lucy claims to have been passively led because it was socially unacceptable for women to "actively pursue their own ends except through marriage" (294), and Lucy is a conventional girl in many ways. For example, even though she realizes that she has a gift for acting, she would never consider attempting an acting career, like Vashti, who has sold her soul and her respectability for her art.

Lucy is content with the most menial work because "it seemed to me a great thing to be without heavy anxiety, and relieved from intimate trial; the negation of severe suffering was the nearest approach to happiness I expected to know" (140). Lucy dares not even hope for a better future, as if daring to hope is an invitation to Fate to knock her down. Life is "a hopeless desert," and she "dared not hope" because she fears "the sin and weakness of presumption" (228). Unlike Jane Eyre, she scarcely seems to have the will to live. Critic Robert Keefe attributes Lucy's deep depression to the guilt of the survivor, with its accompanying desire to die, and he feels that Lucy's mental state is similar to Charlotte Brontë's after the deaths of all her siblings.

Lucy needs the company of others, yet she also dreads it. She despises the constant stream of half-truths and lies that keep social interactions flowing among the girls and women at the Rue Fossette. Her past seems to have made her incapable of forming easy friendships, because there is so much she is unwilling to reveal about herself, yet she suffers acutely from her isolation and loneliness. She prefers to be alone because in unfamiliar company, "a wretched idiosyncracy" practically paralyzes her (274). Alone, she indulges in the most humorous and ironic reveries, as when she describes the Rubenesque painting of Cleopatra (275), yet in company she can barely speak. The real Lucy is hidden from view, frozen inside an icy shell. Her greatest desire is to find someone who will melt her armor, get to know who she really is, but this is also her greatest fear. Lucy finally does allow herself to love and trust again, and this is her greatest achievement as a character.

Although Lucy hungers for human companionship, she is never willing to completely give herself to another at the expense of her own integrity. When M. Paul pressures her to convert to Catholicism, she refuses, because "out of men's afflictions and affections were forged the rivets of their servitude" (514). Lucy seems to think that love itself is like the Catholic Church, offering men respite from suffering at the price of their freedom of conscience, and she believes that preserving her freedom and integrity is more important even than love. This fear of dissolution into another's personality is a great barrier between her and others, for she spends a lot of psychic energy just keeping her ego from disintegrating.

Lucy is incapable of asking anyone for help or friendship, or of acting strongly for her own good. The one positive move she does make to see M. Paul—leaving Madame Beck's apartment to be at his farewell reception—is easily foiled by Madame Beck, who simply stands in front of her and begins talking volubly to M. Paul so that he doesn't even notice that Lucy has come. To those critics who see Madame Beck as simply an avatar of Lucy's personality, Madame Beck represents that side of Lucy that represses her emotional nature, freezing any action that is motivated by emotions. Finally, Lucy is "pierced deeper than [she] could endure" when Madame Beck refuses to allow M. Paul to speak to her alone. "My heart will break!" escapes from her lips, the ice has cracked, and M. Paul finally resorts to the unheard of expedient of striking his cousin and employer to get her to leave the room (580).

Lucy's nature is less passive than paralyzed by a self-willed paralysis. She has kept her true nature "in catalepsy and a dead trance" to avoid hoping for anything, and when life springs up within her she has knocked it on the head with a nail through the temples (175–176). The opium administered to her by Madame Beck releases her from her iron self-control and freezing inhibitions and allows her to realize for the first time that she is in a prison of her own making. Her surprisingly easy escape is a great step toward her own self-actualization.

Other than opium, the only thing that can release Lucy from her frozen state is love. She is like Sleeping Beauty awaiting a kiss to awaken her from a deathlike sleep. She believes that women are hardly capable of happiness alone: they must be reflecting the love and appreciation of a man in order to feel happy themselves, and it is only M. Paul who gives her a reason to assert herself to make a living. Her relationship with Paul is like her relationship with God. She describes the torture of suspense, waiting for Paul to come and get her for their interview, a suspense worse than despair, during which she is "trusting" yet at the same time "terribly fearing" (542). She hopes for M. Paul in the same way she hopes for life eternal: "I believe while I tremble; I trust while I weep" (451). Lucy needs someone else to live for, and God is too distant and too inscrutable to satisfy this longing. Her longing for God is only a longing for death, yet longing to die is a sin. M. Paul is her reason to live, to strive and succeed as a schoolmistress. Although fate is still against her, and M. Paul is lost at sea, she has become a stronger character by actively reaching out to another. In the act of writing this narrative, in her old age, when her hair is white with "the frosts of time" (105), Lucy reminds us of Miss Marchmont recalling her one season of happiness followed by a life of misery, who only on her deathbed can say with sincerity, "Inscrutable God, Thy will be done!" (99). Perhaps Lucy has done a great deal of good as mistress of a school and fulfilled her destiny more fully because she has taken chances.

A character who is singularly protected from the types of misfortunes that befall Lucy is Polly Home. While Madame Beck may represent Lucy's repression of the emotional life, Polly represents another option for Lucy in a man-centered world, an option Lucy rejects. Polly chooses to "serve the idol" Graham, while Lucy resents his privileges and unconsciously desires his position of power (Silver 291). When Polly first arrives at the Brettons, Lucy compares her to a doll, and like a doll Polly is fondled and played with by Mrs. Bretton and Graham. Unlike Lucy, Polly has the power to please others. Her father thinks all the world of her, and she amuses and enchants Graham as Lucy has never done nor thought of doing. Lucy thinks Polly's exaggerated imitation of womanliness and her extreme attachments to the men in her life are silly. She worries that Polly will be in for a rude awakening, when in fact the rude awakening is being prepared for Lucy.

When deprived of her father, around whom she had gravitated as a planet orbits the sun, Polly slowly transfers her affection and care to Graham Bretton. Graham and Polly begin a mock courtship that foreshadows their later relationship, and Polly becomes completely absorbed in Graham's world: "With curious readiness did she adapt herself to such themes as interested him. One would have thought the child had no mind or life of her own, but must necessarily live, move, and have her being in another: now that her father was taken from her, she nestled to Graham, and seemed to feel by his feelings: to exist in his existence" (83). While Lucy will spend much of the novel attempting to maintain her ego-integrity, Polly easily forgets herself completely to serve her father or Graham. Lucy refuses to become a satellite to M. Paul in the way Polly is to her father and to Graham.

Polly will never be homeless in the way Lucy is; her last name emphasizes this major difference between the two. Lucy compares the six-year-old Polly to a doll and the adult Polly to a much loved and pampered lapdog. She can show "the spoiled child's wilfulness, and the heiress's imperiousness" (521) without being any less charming or loved by her family and friends. But despite her occasional envy and disdain of the younger girl, Lucy actually likes Polly and feels that they have many similarities. Like Lucy, Polly has a cool exterior "surrounding so much pure, fine flame" (467), although the "hoar-frost" of her outer self-control is not yet solidified into a sheet of ice as it has with Lucy. Many critics feel that Polly is Lucy Snowe's idealized image of herself, even though Lucy disdains Polly's naivete, sheltered life, and lack of a well-developed inner self.

John Graham Bretton is a good match for Polly because they are both good-looking, well off, dearly loved by their parents, sure of their places in the world, and favored by fate. He is fortunate because he is charming, good-looking, cheerful, healthy, and loved, but also because he is a man, and thus can pursue a profession that will support him and his mother in a middle-class lifestyle. As someone who will really experience little suffering (even when he experiences calamities, he will recover quickly from them because of his sunny disposition), he cannot sympathize with Lucy's mental suffering in the way M. Paul can. He is too handsome, too self-satisfied, too vain for Lucy. Most critics assume that Lucy falls in love with Dr. John, even though she is always aware that there is a basic incompatibility of character between them. However, it is possible to interpret Lucy's desperation at losing Dr. John to his being her only friend, her only lifeline to the outside world. "He was as good to me as the well is to the parched wayfarer—as the sun to the shivering jail-bird" (327), she writes, and the implication is that any water will taste sweet when we are dying of thirst. Her desperation is doubly cruel because she realizes that Dr. John is not capable of being a good friend, much less a lover. When she loses his letter and cannot be distracted from her search by the presence of Dr. John himself (327), it is clear that her idealization of Dr. John is more important to her than the man. She had always felt this way about Graham, for when she stayed with her godmother as a fourteen-year-old, she loved to gaze at his portrait (243) but seems to have avoided him in person. When Dr. John turns his attention to Polly, Lucy is devastated because she is again entirely alone and deserted; however, she had always known that he could be unfeelingly faithless, simply because he was so handsome, so admired, and so loved. Graham begins and ends his life favored by fate, because "he was born victor, as some are born vanquished" (529). While M. Paul could not prevail over his fiancée's relatives, Graham easily vanquishes and makes a friend of M. de Bassompierre.

Madame Beck (Modeste Maria Beck) is someone Lucy admires, despises, and hates. Self-interest is her only motivator. She has complete control over her feelings and emotions, mainly because she has few feelings and emotions, as her heart is "impotent and dead" (137). Even when she is disappointed in love, she controls herself admirably, because she is not capable of passion. She is a hard, cold, calculating woman who rules though espionage, surveillance, and deceit. She cannot even muster motherly concern and affection for her own children, although she looks after their best interests as much as she looks after her own.

Lucy admires Madame Beck's good sense, business acumen, and consummate self-control but despises her duplicity and judges her as lacking true feelings and heart. Madame Beck becomes Lucy's rival for M. Paul's hand because, even though she does not love him, she wants to "bind him to her interest" (544). Lucy is capable of discerning as much about Madame Beck's character as Madame Beck is capable of discerning about Lucy's. To Lucy, Madame Beck's outer deportment, her mask, is "a mere network reticulated with holes; and I saw underneath a being heartless, self-indulgent, and ignoble" (544). Because Madame Beck and Lucy seem to intuitively know and understand each other, many critics have seen Madame Beck as an extension of Lucy's personality: "Deep into some of Madame's secrets I had entered—I know not how; by an intuition or an inspiration which came to me—I know not whence" (544). Madame Beck seems to be able to read Lucy Snowe like an open book, and vice versa, although both continually disguise their inner feelings and seem to have little close communication with each other. Lucy has considered becoming like Madame Beck, the mistress of her own school, but despairs that this goal is too cold, selfish, and loveless. However, it is likely that Lucy continued her school after M. Paul's death, and perhaps she became similar to Madame Beck, who, after all, had also lost her husband. Madame Snowe would be as unlikely to share her past tragedies as Madame Beck seems to be. Perhaps Lucy sees in Madame Beck the woman she may be fated to become.

Another character whose ruling passion is selfishness, and who may represent yet another aspect of Lucy's character, is Ginevra Fanshawe. She is a great flirt because she knows that she is noticeably, flashily beautiful. She is not too proud to beg money and items of dress from all her friends and relatives. Her only desire is to enjoy herself. Her only virtue is her blunt, rude honesty with Lucy; she does not flatter or mince words but tells Lucy exactly what she thinks about her friend. Lucy seems inexplicably drawn to Ginevra, and they remain verbal sparring partners and companions until Ginevra elopes. Lucy always chooses to share her food with Ginevra and no other girl, and she lets Ginevra and no other lean on her and extract favors from her. Ginevra seems to be thrust out into the world to find herself a suitable husband, yet she relishes the adventure instead of dreading it. Not protected and coddled like Polly Home, she manages to make the best of circumstances and to think well of herself no matter how others may think of her. Unlike Lucy, she never feels afraid, guilty, undeserving, unlucky, or even upset at receiving sound verbal drubbings from her Diogenes. Lucy admits that Ginevra is very clever about getting what she wants; Lucy admires her resilience and envies her happiness in the same way she envies Polly Home's good fortune.

M. Paul Carlos David Emanuel is a passionate, extroverted, demanding, and comically sincere little man who thinks he has understood Lucy inside and out from the moment of his phrenological assessment on the night she arrived at Madame Beck's. While others see only a "colorless shadow" in Lucy, M. Paul sees "a passionate ardour for triumph" (226), the fire and flame in Lucy's nature. Is he really seeing the true Lucy, or only a reflection of himself? Lucy tells him she values triumph much less than she values a sincere friend, and he offers to be her friend early in the novel.

M. Paul is comically sexist as well, but Lucy may attribute this to his being a Catholic. He believes that men are "the nobler sex" (208) and that presumptuous women such as Lucy "must be kept down" (226). He is enraged when he finds Lucy sitting, alone, in front of the indecent portrait of the Cleopatra and moves her to contemplate a severely conservative series of representations of women. He lends Lucy many books but always tears out any pages that contain material he deems inappropriate for a woman's eye (435). He cannot bear to be bettered by anyone, especially a woman.: "In a love of power, in an eager grasp after supremacy M. Emanuel was like Bonaparte" (438).

He can at times seem very cruel and insensitive, as when he crushes up one of Lucy's elaborate line drawings in his haste to have her prove her talent to his colleagues. The narrator Lucy deprecates her own work, saying that the line drawing was no more valuable than worsted-work, because it was only a copy, but the character Lucy had valued the drawing. Some critics (for example, Kate Millett) feel that M. Paul could never have made a good husband, because he seems to think that anything a woman is scribbling at must be of no value, and that Charlotte Brontë kills him off for the good of her heroine. Other critics feel that M. Paul has changed dramatically by the end of the novel, since he helps Lucy begin her own school, while before he had felt that intellectual women were anathema to male happiness and working women were redundant, as all the important work was being done by males.

M. Paul is as determined to be top dog as Madame Beck, but Lucy can more easily accept his despotism because she feels his talents and abilities give him the undisputed right to leadership. M. Paul is almost like God to Lucy. When his face shines upon her, she is happy, and when he recedes she is in dark despair. For his approval she will work harder at her studies than she has ever worked before. When he offers her a school, he becomes her "king; royal for me had been that hand's bounty; to offer homage was both a joy and a duty" (587). Many critics have noted M. Paul's function as Lucy's savior. Lucy spends her happiest three years waiting for "the second coming of Emanuel" (Boumelha 106). While Jane Eyre had reproved herself for making Rochester her idol, Lucy Snowe never feels this way about M. Paul (although she does feel that Dr. John had become a false idol to her). In *Holy Ghosts: The Male Muses of Charlotte and Emily Brontë*, critic Irene Tayler offers a brilliant reading of *Villette* as a Christian allegory, where John Graham Bretton represents the flesh and Paul Emmanuel represents Christ.

THEMATIC ISSUES

Villette has many themes and many possible interpretations. As in *Jane Eyre* and *Shirley*, "the woman question" is again addressed: how is an unmarried woman to live in such a patriarchal society? Many critics feel that the novel depicts the inner workings of a neurotic mind, while others feel that Lucy succeeds despite her disadvantages and that her "neurosis" is simply a necessary defense. The theme of the orphan again appears, as it has in all Charlotte's novels, with emphasis on exile, homelessness, and a dearth of love. The heroine's plain, unattractive outward appearance is again emphasized, even more than it had been in *Jane Eyre*. A woman's painful confinement in menial, unrewarding work is again a theme, as is the unfair advantages men have over women in the world of work. The themes of surveillance and of camouflage have been widely discussed, as has Lucy's apparently passive nature and use of the passive voice. Religion plays a crucial role again, but here it is Protestantism against Catholicism, rather than tensions between different forms of Protestantism.

The theme of divine justice is handled differently in *Villette* than in Charlotte's previous novels. Hard work, good intentions, and faith do not always lead to rewards in this world, and a lack of these good qualities does not always lead to suffering. Lucy seems to accept and understand that the torments of her life are not the result of her lack of faith. Paulina also understands that the deserving often "die in utter want" while she has been abundantly blessed even though she is "not actively good" (466). At times the entire novel seems to be a meditation on Luke 8:18: "For to him who has will more be given, and from him who has not, even what he thinks that he has will be taken away." In this parable, which is variously interpreted, Jesus says that only those who have faith will understand his parables and thereby receive even greater faith, but those whose faith was weak will lose even that which they thought they had. In other words, if we take advantage of our opportunities, they bring us other and higher opportunities; but if we neglect them, even the initial opportunities are taken away. Lucy seems to ask for so little, yet she never can keep even the little that she is allowed to receive. She does not neglect her opportunities but she cannot seem to profit by them. A favorite for a time at Mrs. Brettons', she finds her place usurped by Polly. After the shipwreck of her family, she clings to Mrs. Marchmont as a source of shelter and stability, only to be driven out into the world again by that lady's death: "My little morsel of human affection, which I prized as if it were a solid pearl, must melt in my fingers and slip thence like a dissolving hailstone" (97). Meanwhile, those who are already loved, and who are already financially secure, find more love and greater financial security, and even the bad and worthless succeed without trouble. Ginevra receives her inheritance even though she has eloped with de Hamal and continues her life "suffering as little as any human being I have ever known" (577), and Madame Beck prospers all the days of her life.

Homelessness and orphanhood are again important themes, as they had been in the previous two novels. Lucy must make her way in the world without a single calling card. She feels a profound sense of homelessness, exacerbated but also symbolized by her residence in Labassecour. Lucy can survive by wit and hard work alone, but she cannot achieve true happiness without a family for whom to work. Because she is an orphan, in a foreign country, no one knows who Lucy really is, and she feels that they can never truly know her. Different people perceive her completely differently, but she does nothing to correct their misapprehensions.

Lucy prefers to remain camouflaged because she takes a perverse pleasure in remaining ignored where she "can never be rightly known" (164). The theme of camouflaging the self is much more developed in *Villette* than elsewhere. Lucy does not reveal her true feelings because she feels "too perverse to defend herself" from others' misjudgments and imputations (427). Lucy feels comfortable when she is as inconspicuous as possible, because human contact is painful to one who is always misjudged. Only M. Paul seems to realize that she has a burning soul, and he easily sees through her shadowy, quiet, and grave exterior.

One reason that Lucy prefers to remain camouflaged is that her present financial position does not reflect the social class she was born into. Ambiguous social class and the descent from the class of one's birth are again important themes, because class is indicative of much more than wealth. When she is treated rudely by the maidservant and the waiters at the London hotel, she reminds the waiter that he knows her uncles, because Lucy wants to be treated with the respect due to her class. When Lucy goes out in her opium-induced state, she feels at home with both middle- and working-class citizens, but when completely sober, she is always mortified to be taken as a working-class woman or a servant.

Lucy's ambiguous social class isolates her from others, and the themes of isolation and loneliness are more pronounced here than in Charlotte's previous novels. Lucy chooses to be alone rather than with people who can never understand her or whom she feels are not sympathetic to her nature. She finds the other teachers to be narrow, coarse egoists who are corrupt, avaricious, or otherwise not compatible; therefore it is a waste of her time and energy to socialize with them. She rejects the meaningless togetherness of the common herd, but she suffers extremely for this isolation during the long vacation.

Lucy's position as an unmarried woman of ambiguous class is symbolized by the themes of being buried alive by circumstances and of being frozen into lifelessness. Her anomalous position in the social world makes her afraid to hope, afraid even to feel: "About the present, it was better to be stoical: about the future—such a future as mine—to be dead. And in catalepsy and a dead trance, I studiously held the quick of my nature" (175). Her entire being is held in a deadly self-constraint. At times when she longs for something more, she knocks the longings on the head, "driving a nail through their temples" (176). She is continually killing her inner spirit in order to live, zombielike, in the body.

Lucy believes that her circumstances demand self-negation, because reason tells her there is nothing to hope for. The conflict between reason and the imagination is a theme that appears in all Charlotte's novels, but here imagination is kept in much sterner check. Reason is a harsh mistress that offers only "the gnawed bone dogs had forsaken." Only imagination sweetens such a life, appeasing this famine with food "sweet and strange" (308). If it were not for her imagination, Lucy feels that she would die, yet she constantly suppresses it, convinced that it will lead her astray and give her false hopes.

Lucy feels that she has no reason to hope for love because she is not attractive, and the lack of outward beauty in a world that judges everyone by appearance alone is again an important theme. When she catches sight of herself in a mirror at the concert hall, the image causes "a jar of discord, a pang of regret; it was not flattering" (286). Lucy feels that beauty is capable of loving only itself (287), but she admires beauty in others because beauty has the ability to please. Lucy is just as charmed as Dr. John is by Ginevra's beauty, because Ginevra more than anyone else has the power to please others through her looks alone. Lucy mourns her plain exterior because she has "a great fear of displeasing" (583) those she loves, and she asks M. Paul pointedly if her appearance displeases his eyes much, but he replies in such a way to silence her worries. M. Paul has seen her inner beauty and value and is not at all repulsed by her outward form, much as Jane and Rochester completely disregard their respective physical defects in their perfect mental and spiritual union.

Because Lucy is not beautiful, she fears that she will have to support herself, and the theme of employment for women is central in *Villette*, as it had been in *Shirley* and *Jane Eyre*. Lucy's choices of occupation are companion to a wealthier woman, child nurse, and teacher. They offer very little money for constant work and surveillance, as all require living in. Lucy pursues a career because she must, but she gets little enjoyment out of her teaching job, even though she does it well. When she looks forward to starting her own school, she sees her financial independence as only a stepping stone to what she really wants. Working is not a privilege for Lucy but is instead a painful necessity, and she is not the only teacher at the Rue Fossette who would gladly lay her burden down. Many of the teachers are in debt and dream of being rescued by marriage.

The theme of romantic love dominates *Villette*, and we see love between incompatible people, unrequited love, love comparable to idol worship, maternal love for a son and paternal love for a daughter, and also love that completes and makes whole. The theme of melancholy also pervades the work, and even true love cannot cure melancholy, as we see by the king and queen of Labassecour. Lucy and Ginevra offer contrasting pictures of disposition. Lucy is melancholy by nature. An unexpected event can make her happy for a while, but she doesn't believe that happiness can last; the best she can hope for is to keep sadness at bay for a time (334). Ginevra is cheerful by nature. An unexpected disappointment can make her unhappy for a few moments, but she quickly bounces back to cheerfulness, because she doesn't believe that anything really can go wrong for her, or that other people really believe she has all the faults they say she has.

HISTORICAL/SOCIAL-CULTURAL CONTEXTS

The Roman Catholic Church is severely criticized in this novel. The pious lectures delivered every night are "mainly designed as a wholesome mortification of the Intellect, a useful humiliation of the Reason; and such a dose for Common Sense as she might digest at her leisure, and thrive on as she best could" (184). In other words, no one with intelligence, reason, or common sense could take seriously the outlandishly fictional tales of the Catholic saints and martyrs that are the subjects of these pious lectures. The Roman Catholic Church rears its children to be "fat, ruddy, hale, joyous, ignorant, unthinking, unquestioning" (196). Lucy compares the Roman Catholic Church to Satan, to an idol the people worship that keeps them from knowing Christ.

Because the Pope would not annul his marriage to Catherine of Aragon, Henry VIII forced a break with Rome in 1534. The king of England became the titular head of the Anglican or established church. Since that time, the Church of England has been the country's national church, with a long-standing suspicion of the Roman Catholic Church on political rather than theological grounds. Since a Roman Catholic would owe primary allegiance to the Pope in Rome rather than to the king or queen of England, converting to Catholicism, to many Englishmen, was practically an act of treason. The Oxford Movement was begun at Oxford in 1833 as a reform of the Church of England, moving it back in the direction of Roman Catholicism. The Oxford Movement encouraged Rome to step up its evangelism in England, hoping to win as many converts as possible. One of the founders of the movement, the distinguished scholar and minister of the Church of England, John Henry Newman, became a Catholic cardinal. *Villette* is in a sense Charlotte's commentary on the Oxford Movement, just as *Shirley* had been her commentary on the Luddite movement.

Catholicism is mixed with the theme of "foreignness" to describe the character of the Labassecoureans, who are described as intellectually lazy and deceitful. Lucy consistently refers to everyone at the school as "foreigners," even though *she* is the foreigner, not they. The British chauvinism that characterizes even Lucy's lack of self-esteem reflects the fact that Britain was a world empire in the mid-nineteenth century, engaged in an imperialistic expansion of its colonies and provinces all over the globe. To the Brontës and their contemporaries, Britain was the obvious center of the world.

The defeat of Napoleon Bonaparte, at Waterloo in Belgium in 1815, left the British the strongest military power on earth, directly or indirectly controlling about one-fourth of the world's land and people. During the Napoleonic Wars, Napoleon I was the most hated man in England. Yet Lucy seems to admire some of Napoleon Bonaparte's characteristics, such as his strength of character and his charismatic leadership. Several times, Lucy compares M. Paul to Napoleon Bonaparte. Like Napoleon, M. Paul is short, energetic, ambitious, an inspirational leader, one who likes to command, hates to praise, and cares nothing for the social graces. The chauvinistic tone Lucy sometimes adopts can be related to the renewed revolutions on the continent during the mid-century, including Louis Napoleon's coup d'état of December 1851, which temporarily renewed British fears of a French invasion.

The Dutch-speaking natives of Belgium, known as the Flemish, have produced many great artists, one of the best known being Peter Paul Rubens (1577–1640). The Cleopatra painting Lucy sardonically admires is meant to remind us of a Rubens painting. Although Rubens never painted a Cleopatra, he was famous for his fleshy women and for the vast scale of his paintings. Vashti is based on one of the most famous actresses of the nineteenth century, a Frenchwoman named Rachel.

Villette presents examples of successful professional women such as Vashti and Madame Beck, but both portraits are ambiguous. Vashti is a great artist, yet the world (epitomized by Dr. John) judges her as a failed woman, someone who has lived an immoral life and is now dying an unrepentant death. Madame Beck is a failure as a woman also, since she cannot love even her own children. Lucy is torn between the desire for a career and the desire for a fulfilling relationship. Although early feminists demanded that women have access to careers, teaching was not really considered a career. The early feminists tended to be middle-class women who were expected to marry and who resented the boring life they could expect to lead as wives. However, with no family and no dowry, marriage seems like a hopelessly impossible dream for Lucy, not the expected course of her life. Earning a living is therefore not a choice, but is forced upon her by a cruel fate.

Well-paying careers for women were almost nonexistent. A great artist or author might make a living, but the average woman could not be educated into a well-paying career, as Dr. John has been. Women were paid only subsistence wages, as Charlotte discovered while a teacher and a governess. Men doing the same work, as professors or tutors, earned much more. While Charlotte had ended her previous novels with the heroine's marriage, here she leaves Lucy to her fate as the head of her own school, but the triumph seems cold and bitter. However, Charlotte Brontë clearly rejected the prescribed role of Victorian woman as "the Angel in the House," an ideal she mocks in the character of Polly Home. "The Angel in the House" is a concept first developed in a popular poem by Coventry Patmore titled "The Rose of the World" (1854–1856), which describes the ideal Victorian woman as a perfect wife and mother whose only desire is to please her husband. The same sentiment is expressed by many other Victorian writers, including John Ruskin in "Of Queen's Gardens" and Sarah Stickney Ellis in *Wives of England*.

LITERARY DEVICES AND CRAFT

One of the most striking stylistic characteristics of *Villette* is the use of extended metaphors that often entirely replace the facts to which they refer. For example, Lucy compares the tragedy that befell her family after she left the Brettons' to a shipwreck. The extended metaphor, which begins with Lucy supposedly sunbathing on the deck and ends with shipwreck and the death of all aboard except the narrator (94), entirely conceals the true nature of the tragedy. In realistic fiction, metaphor usually elaborates on the facts rather than completely substituting for them. Here, the emotional impact of the events is more important than the events themselves; it is, in fact, all that is left of them.

Another important stylistic innovation is the narrator's relationship with her readers, whom she identifies as complacent, happy, fortunate, and conservative—thus incapable of comprehending the story of Lucy Snowe. The narrator Lucy implies rather than states that her life has not followed the normal course of "la vie de un femme." Of her youth she writes, "A great many women and girls are supposed to pass their lives" basking on the deck of their family ship, so "why not I with the rest? Picture me then idle, basking, plump, and happy, stretched on a cushioned deck" (94). The conventional, unimaginative reader is invited to picture Lucy's youth as spent in the conventional way, because "the amiable conjecture does no harm," yet a far different and far less pleasant reality is implied, one that does not fit into the conventional pattern and is therefore non-narratable. Similarly, the fate of M. Paul's ship is left unspecified, although clearly implied, so as to "leave sunny imaginations hope" (596). The narrator Lucy Snowe stops short of sharing deep griefs with the reader just as Lucy the character has with the other characters, but this very refusal to use melodramatic, sensational description creates the intended feeling of bleak despair by denying the reader his visceral, voyeuristic gratification in gory detail.

Another important characteristic of the style is its wit and irony. Lucy is a highly ironical and at times sardonic narrator. The best example of the wittily ironic style is Lucy's description of the painting of Cleopatra (275–276), but many other examples can be found. The last paragraph of the novel is an example of the bitter irony that is also characteristic of many other sections.

As in her other novels, Charlotte personifies concepts such as reason, imagination, and hope. Reason and imagination fight duels over her soul, with reason being an unbearably harsh mistress and imagination offering little more than fool's gold. Allusions to the Bible and to Bunyan's *Pilgrim's Progress* are again abundant here, as they were in *Jane Eyre*. Lucy's allusions to the Bible often express her anguish, as when she knocks her desires on the head "after the manner of Jael to Sisera, driving a nail through their temples" (176), or when she sees M. Paul and the young Justine Marie at the park: "I invoked Conviction to nail upon me the certainty, abhorred while embraced, to fix it with the strongest spikes her strongest strokes could drive; and when the iron had entered well my soul, I stood up, as I thought, renovated" (566). Lucy is crucifying herself by making herself believe that Paul loves Justine Marie. She hopes to be "renovated" by this crucifixion, born again, transfigured into a new person who is not susceptible to romantic delusions, who is free from emotional pain and torment, but the crucifixion is unsuccessful. Images of mutilation, death, and being buried alive abound, as when Lucy must leave the Rue Fossette whose roof is "crushing as the slab of a tomb" (232). Allusions to Shakespeare's *A Midsummer Night's Dream* in Volume II point to a mismatch of love objects

(Lucy and Dr. John; Dr. John and Ginevra), and Lucy's collapse in the stormy streets outside the church, which ends Volume I, seems to allude to *King Lear*, to the "poor, forked animal" stripped of all supports.

Symbolism is less pronounced here than in *Jane Eyre*, yet the most obvious symbol, that of the nun, has been variously interpreted. After describing the legend of the nun, Lucy calls it "romantic rubbish"—but then she almost immediately sees the nun, so the nun may represent her inability to completely bury her romantic nature.

The nun appears to Lucy five times, and several critics feel that these are times of intense stress in Lucy's life. Clearly, the nun functions on several levels. Like the nun, Lucy feels buried alive at the pensionnate, but what vow has she broken? Is it the vow to live like a nun, as an unmarried woman is supposed to do, devoting herself only to good works and to God? The nun appears to Lucy for the first time as she is about to read a letter from Dr. John, perhaps as a warning to maintain her monastic coolness. Later, the nun appears after Lucy has buried Dr. John's letters in the garden, and we learn that M. Paul has also seen the nun when he reveals that he has also buried a love. While Lucy never doubts her own sanity, she does seem to entertain the idea that the nun may be a visitant from a spiritual realm, come to reveal some message to her. Lucy last sees the nun after she returns from the carnival, believing that M. Paul will surely marry his ward. The nun suggests re*nun*ciation of earthly love and earthly hope, yet the nun turns out to be not only a humbug, but also a disguise that hides the illicit and very earthly love between de Hamal and Ginevra. The nun must die if Lucy and M. Paul are to believe in the possibility of earthly happiness. Even though their happiness is fated to be very short, it was right for both of them, although all the forces of tradition, Catholicism, patriarchy, and fortune were against them.

The other obvious symbolism is that of names. Lucy Snowe's name symbolizes her cool, icy reserve, a reserve that Charlotte claimed not to admire. Polly Home's name suggests that she will always have a home, unlike the homeless Lucy. John Bretton's name suggests Britain, and he is the epitome of a complacent, self-absorbed Englishman. Between them, Dr. Bretton and Polly Home lock Lucy out of both Britain and home. M. Emanuel's name suggests his role as Lucy's savior. The country of Labassecour humorously suggests "the farmyard" in French, suggesting the animal as opposed to spiritual quality of the inhabitants.

Doubled characters also play an important role, as they did in *Jane Eyre* and *Shirley*. Ginevra and Lucy are opposites of each other, but in many ways Ginevra is Lucy's alter ego. Lucy is afraid to ask for anything, but Ginevra is never shy in asking or taking. Lucy is quiet and shadowy, while Ginevra is brilliant. Lucy always gives half of her rolls to Ginevra at breakfast and likes "to let her take the lion's share, whether of the white beer, the sweet wine, or the new milk" (313). She feels that Ginevra deserves the greatest part of pleasure in the world simply because she is beautiful, as if the law of nature decrees that Ginevra flourish while Lucy fades away.

Polly is also very similar to Lucy and may be another side of her ego. Like Lucy, Polly is intelligent and sincere, with a cool exterior hiding an inner flame. When Graham writes her a letter, she trembles as much as Lucy did to open her letter from Graham, and like Lucy, she writes several drafts of her reply, "chastening and subduing the phrases at every rescript" (466). Paulina is not stronger or better than Lucy, only luckier. "Much pain, much fear, much struggle" would have destroyed Paulina's outward beauty, as well as her health, her cheerfulness, her grace, and her sweetness (467). Instead, fate has chosen Lucy to be the victim of such circumstances, and these unfavorable, unlucky circumstances have made Lucy harder, colder, more reserved, and more cynical than she otherwise would have been.

Madame Beck also represents a side of Lucy's character, the side of iron self-control. Lucy admires Madame Beck's self-control but is horrified by her coldness, duplicity, and lack of any motivation save self-interest. While Polly represents what Lucy could have been had she been more fortunate, Madame Beck represents what Lucy may become if she kills all her imaginative and moral qualities in the interests of self-control, self-restraint, and self-preservation.

Foreshadowing is another literary device that Brontë uses effectively. Lucy's life of struggle begins with the extended metaphor of a shipwreck, which foreshadows the shipwreck at the end of the novel that destroys her hopes and wrecks her chances of a home again. Miss Marchmont's story of a blissful engagement ending with the tragic and violent death of the fiancé also foreshadows Paul's death and perhaps alludes to Lucy's future life as well. The structure represented by these foreshadowings is circular, representing an endless cycle of hope followed by despair. Lucy compares herself to Moses in the wilderness (309), who died without being allowed to enter the Promised Land, being offered only a view of it before he died. This foreshadows Paul's expected return after a three-year absence. Lucy is offered a glimpse of the earthly promised land she will never be allowed to enter. However, if we read Paul Emanuel as Christ, then Lucy has gained spiritual salvation at the cost of worldly bliss.

ALTERNATIVE PERSPECTIVE: PSYCHOLOGICAL CRITICISM

Psychological literary criticism has its origins with Sigmund Freud (1856–1939), the Austrian physician who invented psychoanalysis. A practicing neurologist, Freud began to search for the psychological roots of physical symptoms that had no known physical cause, and he came to believe that the unconscious mind was responsible for symptoms and behaviors that could not otherwise be explained. Freud's theories have had an enormous effect on many fields, including the analysis of literature, since Freud himself admitted gaining insight into psychological universals by studying literature. For example, the Oedipus complex, in which a son incestuously loves his mother and wishes to murder his father, is illustrated in Shakespeare's *Hamlet*. Freud theorized that underneath a veneer of language and civilization, people are governed by basic drives—the sexual and the aggressive drives. The mind, for Freud, is composed of the id, ego, and superego. The id is a cauldron of seething desires, often contradicting each other, but the id knows nothing of logic, law, morals, and consequences. The ego mediates between the outside world and the id, acting as a reality check to the amoral desires of the id, while the superego demands of the ego an even stricter repression of behavior according to idealistic social norms. If the ego fails to live up to these impossible ideals, it is punished by a sense of inferiority and guilt. Even the book's earliest critics have seen in Lucy Snowe a veneer of extreme repression covering up equally extreme sexual and aggressive drives. Matthew Arnold, in 1853, wrote that in *Villette* he saw nothing but "hunger, rebellion, and rage" (Allott 93).

In *Civilization and Its Discontents*, Freud theorized that a complex, advanced civilization forced excessive inhibition of the sexual and aggressive drives, leading to neurosis. In *Beyond the Pleasure Principle*, he theorized the existence of the death drive—the wish to return to a state of nonconsciousness—to explain behavior that could not be motivated by either the sexual or the aggressive drives. Some critics think Lucy Snowe is the finest representation of neurosis in the history of literature, while others have noted her desire to die.

Besides analyzing characters, Freudian literary criticism often psychoanalyzes the novelist herself, to understand how her unconscious drives may have shaped her narrative. Since *Villette* is partially based on Charlotte's experience in Brussels, and M. Paul is clearly modeled on her beloved professor M. Heger, even many of the earliest critics felt that the novel was a thinly veiled autobiography.

Jacques Lacan, the best-known recent Freudian theorist, combines semiotics (the philosophical theory of signs, symbols, and language systems) and psychoanalytical theory to emphasize the role language plays in the subconscious mind. Language always represents something that is absent, and consciousness itself, according to both Freud and Lacan, begins with this sense of absence. For Freud, it is the physical (temporary) absence of the mother, but Lacan elaborates on this sense of loss by showing how consciousness of self represents the child's loss of the feeling that it is as important to its mother as its mother is to it. When the baby realizes he is a completely separate being from the mother, he also realizes that he does not completely fulfill his mother's desires. This feeling of loss first occurs during what Lacan calls "the mirror-stage," that stage in development when the infant first realizes that the image he sees in the mirror is *himself.* The image in the mirror is complete and whole, while the desiring subject who views the image feels much less than complete and whole. The desiring subject becomes alienated from his image of himself. He then enters the realm of the symbolic, where one thing (such as a mirror image) represents another. Entering the symbolic realm essentially makes us human, but it also thrusts us into the realm of "the law of the Father," where words are more powerful than instincts and the desire to be that perfect image in the mirror (the idealized self) creates endless frustration and even a desire to die (Lacan 42). Lucy seems to have a very strict ideal image of herself—the image of a person with perfect self-control. Yet her desire for life breaks through, and the combat between her ego ideal and her passions often leads to despair.

Lucy also despairs of ever being truly known by another human being. There are several scenes where Lucy sees her reflection in a mirror and doesn't recognize herself at first, and she then feels totally alienated from her image, as if that image and her ego had nothing in common. "The first object of desire is to be recognized by the other" (58), writes Lacan, and to be recognized by another is probably necessary to biological life itself. Even lower forms of life like locusts and pigeons cannot develop properly if separated from others of their species, and other researchers have shown that infants and young children need loving attention to survive: with just food, water, and shelter, they will die. Since losing her berth on the middle-class ship of life, Lucy knows that her inner self is constantly being misjudged by her outer appearance, dress, and occupations. Even her godmother and John Bretton completely fail to recognize who she really is. Because she feels that those who once loved her and who are now dead are the only ones who really knew her, Lucy's nightmare of long-dead relatives being alienated from her is truly horrific, making death itself seem like no relief from suffering. She is driven to confess in a Catholic Church partly because of the fear and despair experienced in this nightmare and partly because "she is almost desperate to be the focus of someone else's gaze" (Wolstenholme 62). The Catholic confessional is very similar to the psychoanalyst's couch, and the Protestant Lucy is drawn to the confessional as a few decades later suffering patients would be drawn into psychoanalysis, where by telling their story to another human being, they are relieved of the intolerable feeling of being unknown and unrecognized for who they think they are. It is easy to see why *Villette* has often been analyzed using different types of psychoanalytic criticism.

The Professor
(1857)

The Professor, completed in 1846, was intended to be Charlotte's first published novel. However, it was rejected by publisher after publisher. Even after the phenomenal success of *Jane Eyre* and *Shirley,* Charlotte's publisher, Smith and Elder, still declined to publish it. The public, wrote Charlotte in her 1851 preface to *The Professor* (written for the unsuccessful resubmission of the manuscript), has "a passionate preference for the wild, wonderful, and thrilling—the strange, startling, and harrowing" (xxiii), and also for beautiful heroines, dashing heroes, unexpected inheritances, and fairy-tale endings. *The Professor* has none of these. Charlotte consciously chose to write a realistic, unexciting novel about an ordinary, unexciting hero because she wished to say good-bye to her adolescent style of writing in which evil, dashing heroes commit murder, adultery, and political intrigue, while their wives, concubines, and mistresses live only for their faithless men.

 The Professor was not published during Charlotte's lifetime. After her death, her husband, Arthur Bell Nicholls, did not want it published, because he felt it covered essentially the same material as *Villette.* However, Elizabeth Gaskell, Charlotte's first biographer, finally convinced Mr. Nicholls to release the manuscript, which Smith and Elder published to profit from the fanatical interest generated by the morbid and tragic lives of the Brontë sisters, now all dead.

 The plot is based on Charlotte's experiences as a pupil and a teacher at the Heger's boarding school in Brussels. Her unrequited love for her professor M.

Heger, her aloofness from and disdain of the other pupils, and her anger at Heger's wife Zoë all find expression in her first novel. Crimsworth's rejection of Zoraïde and pursuit of the forlorn and betrayed Frances, ending in their marriage, writes a happy ending for Charlotte's unhappy passion. Zoraïde is a savage portrait of Zoë Heger; William Crimsworth has some characteristics of M. Constantine Heger but also of Charlotte herself; Frances plays the part of Charlotte cruelly torn from her life's love. Charlotte uses a male first-person narrator to distance herself from the narrative and to gain some artistic control over her most personal and heartbreaking experiences. However, this narrative device is not entirely successful, since the protagonist, William Crimsworth, is in many ways an unattractive character. Although an orphan and a victim, like all of Charlotte's heroines, he is cold, cruel, conceited, and priggish.

PLOT DEVELOPMENT

The novel opens as a letter written by the main character, William Crimsworth, to an old school friend he has not seen in ten years. By the end of the first chapter, however, Crimsworth has abandoned the idea of continuing his letter and decides to write to a wider public. William's father, a bankrupt manufacturer, died before he was born, and his mother, a woman of noble blood cut off by her family for marrying a tradesman, died giving birth to William. William and his older brother Edward were raised by their paternal relatives until these relatives were able to blackmail the wealthy maternal side of the family into helping support the children. William was then sent to Eton, a distinguished boys' boarding school. However, Edward was already nineteen years old, so he ended up going into the manufacturing business like his father.

Having received an aristocrat's education, William is offered a position in the church by his maternal uncle, Lord Tynedale, with the understanding that he will marry one of his cousins, daughters of his uncle the Hon. John Seacombe. Crimsworth refuses this offer, feeling no calling for the church, no love for any of his cousins, and no sympathy from his proud relatives, who openly show their contempt for William's father and his line of work. Overreacting to their contempt, William decides to be a tradesman and applies for a position with his elder brother Edward.

Edward has married a wealthy mill owner's daughter and revived his father's business as well, but he still harbors a bitter resentment against William for having been raised as a gentleman at the expense of his hated uncles. William accepts a position translating German and French business letters at his brother's wool warehouse and steels himself against his brother's cruel, arrogant behavior. Treated more like a slave than a brother or even an employee, William bears all with unruffled, haughty coolness, but he finally reaches his limit when his brother accuses him of slander and threatens to horsewhip him. Yorke Hunsden, a manufacturer but also the descendant of wealthy landowners, precipitates the crisis between William and Edward. Hunsden suggests that William go to Europe, and he writes a letter of introduction for him to a Mr. Brown in Belgium, who always has several different employment opportunities at his disposal.

William leaves for Belgium the next day, introduces himself to Mr. Brown, and decides on the spur of the moment to be a teacher, because he hates working in the business world and a position as teacher is available. Mr. Brown introduces him to Monsieur Pelet, the director of a boys' school, who hires him as English and Latin teacher. William's room at the school has a window, boarded up, which had offered a view into the garden of an adjoining girls' boarding school. Disappointed that he cannot see this Garden of Eden, he listens instead, only to be surprised at the girls' rough and unladylike screeching.

Soon he is offered an additional teaching position in the adjoining girls' boarding school, which is directed by Mademoiselle Zoraïde Reuter. The rude, lewd, intellectually inferior and rebellious students at Mlle Reuter's establishment soon dash his ideals of perfect womanhood. Mlle Reuter tries, and soon succeeds, in finding William's weak spot—his sentimental idealism concerning women and love. She almost succeeds in making William fall in love with her. M. Pelet insinuates that Mlle Reuter, if not one of her students, could be persuaded to marry a young man like William. William is morally outraged by the suggestion that he seduce one of his students. He is even more outraged when he learns, by accidentally overhearing their conversation below his window late one night, that M. Pelet and Mlle Reuter are engaged to be married, and that Pelet has been trying to test Zoraïde's faithfulness.

Pelet abuses Zoraïde for flirting with an unattractive, greenhorn schoolboy, but she is pleased to have made her conquest. William gives Pelet the cold shoulder and directly accosts Zoraïde with his knowledge of her engagement. Zoraïde is even more attracted to William because he now treats her with disdain.

Crimsworth becomes fascinated by one of his students, Frances Henri. She teaches lace mending and sewing at the school, and she has asked permission to attend Mr. Crimsworth's English classes. She has a purer English accent than any of his other non-English students, her writing is imaginative, and she takes a real interest in completing his assignments well—unlike the other students, who do as little as possible to get by. He starts to talk to Frances after class, which amazes the students, teachers, and the directress.

Zoraïde asks Crimsworth not to make so much of Frances, since she is not really a student at the school, but a poor, insignificant lace mender. Soon after, Frances stops attending class, and Crimsworth learns that she will not be back. He asks for, then demands, her address from Zoraïde, but she calmly lies by telling him she has never had it. Even though Zoraïde treats Crimsworth like "the great Mogul," her jealousy will not allow her to reveal where Frances lives. William is so enraged and disgusted that he resigns his position at her school.

Crimsworth spends four weeks searching for Frances through the streets of Brussels, and he finally finds her at the Protestant cemetery, grieving for her deceased aunt. She explains how Mlle Reuter let her go while she was taking a short leave to care for her sick aunt. Realizing that he is in love with and wishes to marry her, Crimsworth for the first time regrets his financial position in the world, and he vows to remedy the situation so that he can propose to Frances.

However, he has already resigned his position at Mlle Reuter's, and now that Mlle Reuter and Pelet have set a wedding date, Crimsworth fears that living in the same house with Zoraïde can only lead to his having an affair with the lady. Despite his desire to raise his position in the world, he resigns his position at Pelet's as well, after wrestling with temptation and the spirit of evil, and now he must find a new position in Brussels.

Yorke Hunsden finds him in his rented rooms and informs him that Edward has declared bankruptcy and Crimsworth Hall has been sold. William inquires about the portrait of his mother, but Hunsden mocks his poverty and his sentimentality. The next day, however, the portrait arrives, along with a jeering note from Hunsden that spoils the pleasure William feels in owning the portrait.

Crimsworth appeals to the wealthy, influential father of a former pupil, who recommends him for several positions. Though none of these materialize, he applies everywhere so assiduously that his persistence and reputation finally land him an excellent position at a college. He immediately runs to tell Frances the news and to propose marriage. Frances, who has recently found employment as a teacher, accepts on the condition that she can continue working. After failing to persuade her to be his dependent, he agrees. However, his nerves are so overwrought from all the anxiety and excitement of the past several weeks that he dreams of death and falls into a deep depression, which he calls hypochondria (190). This description of his two-week bout with melancholy seems strangely inserted just at the point of his greatest happiness.

Soon Crimsworth has another visit from Hunsden. At first Hunsden is appalled that Crimsworth is marrying a working-class girl, but after spending an evening with her in spirited debate, he changes his mind and almost envies Crimsworth his luck at finding a compatible mate. Their evening at Frances Henri's ends in a physical wrestling match on the street, with Crimsworth prevailing. Hunsden has no more power over Crimsworth since the latter has found love.

After Crimsworth and Frances marry, Crimsworth continues as professor at his college and Frances at her teaching position. Finding, however, that in a year and a half his salary has risen to nearly eight times her own, Frances determines she must open her own school. Her school is a success. Both work hard and live frugally, invest their money wisely, and are able in ten years to retire from business to live in England. They acquire a small house near the ancient mansion of their friend Hunsden, who has remained a bachelor and inherited the family estate.

The book ends with another unusual scene. Crimsworth's only child Victor has a pet mastiff, given him by Hunsden, which he adores. Hearing that the mastiff has been bitten by a rabid dog, Crimsworth immediately goes into the yard and shoots the mastiff. Victor sees his father kill his beloved pet and is horrified as well as distraught. Crimsworth explains that the mastiff had to be shot, or he would have suffered a terrible death. Because he is his father's son, Victor is calmed by this reasonable explanation, even though he continues to mourn his pet. Reason has prevailed over passion. Similarly, both parents decide to send Victor to boarding school, knowing that they will miss him greatly and that he will be miserable there, because he must experience harsh discipline to curb his ardent temper. Just as his father has prospered not only despite of, but because of the hardships experienced at Eton and with his brother, Victor must also suffer, in order to be "grounded radically in the art of self-control" (221).

CHARACTER DEVELOPMENT

William Crimsworth, the narrator and protagonist, is a young, well-educated, but poor Englishman who must make his own way in the world. He has inherited more traits from his mother, the aristocrat, than from his father, the man of business. He is sensitive, well mannered, and more idealistic than worldly. He refuses a good position in the church simply because he feels no calling and marriage with a wealthy cousin simply because he doesn't love her—both idealistic reasons that would not have deterred a practical-minded nineteenth-century Englishman.

William prides himself on being an intellectual. Sensuous pleasures are not enough for him, and he envies neither his brother Edward's wealth nor his beautiful but infantile wife. Sensual pleasures are usually not "reasonable," and William believes that reason must always prevail over passion. In this he differs from Hunsden, who permits no barriers to intervene "between him and his convenience or pleasure" (20).

If reason is always to prevail over passion, one must practice self-control, and William is proud of his almost complete self-control over his emotions and actions. His coolness and calm under intense pressures drive his brother Edward, and his employer Zoraïde Reuter, to distraction. Hunsden also does everything he can to shake William's composure, but William never reveals in the other man's presence how Hunsden has insulted or hurt him. William sends his son Victor to school to expose him to the kind of hard discipline that he considers necessary to curb Victor's spirit and "ground him radically in the art of self-control" (221).

William values freedom, independence, and integrity. He feels like a slave working for Edward, but he endures as a matter of pride until Hunsden steps in and enrages his brother against him to the point where pride itself mandates his quitting. He resigns from Mlle Reuter's when she refuses to give him Frances's address, and when Zoraïde and Pelet marry, he resigns from M. Pelet's in order to remove himself as a target of Zoraïde's lust.

Before leaving for Belgium, William idealizes women because he has never known any. He interacts with no women while living in England because he feels certain of being repulsed, being neither handsome nor rich. He looks forward to teaching at a girls' boarding school so that he can "gaze both upon the angels and their Eden" (59), and he is offended by M. Pelet's callous and cold manner of referring to the fair sex. However, his views of the opposite sex change remarkably after working at Mlle Reuter's establishment. Except for Frances Henri, no woman escapes his bitter, satiric criticism. Crimsworth's tirades about the flirtatious, seductive, lewd, dishonest and ignorant students at Mlle Reuter's reflect Charlotte's own attitudes toward the female Belgian students and teachers she encountered. Charlotte often represents other women as being every woman's worst enemy. Fortunately Crimsworth ends the novel teaching at a men's college, married to the only woman who meets his standards.

Crimsworth is also humorously chaste and priggish. He is disgusted by M. Pelet's allusions to former love affairs as well as offended by Pelet's sarcastic references to "the fair sex." He differs markedly, even comically, in morals and values from his continental associates, and he often doesn't know what to expect, as, for example, when he fears that Madame Pelet, his employer's old mother, is going to try to seduce him. He firmly resists every attempt Zoraïde makes to seduce him before she is married, yet he leaves Pelet's establishment when Zoraïde marries Pelet because he is sure that "if I stayed, the probability was that, in three months' time, a practical modern French novel would be in full process of concoction under the roof of the unsuspecting Pelet" (154).

His treatment of Frances Henri is partly modeled on Charlotte's memory of M. Heger, who often harangued Charlotte mercilessly only because he perceived her talent. Crimsworth often seems cruel to Frances. He refuses to compliment her when she deserves and expects a compliment; he calls her aside to level numerous criticisms of her work, even though he himself admires it. He tells her that lace mending is "a dull, stupid occupation" (134) before he asks her if she likes her work, and he tells her that she is "a most unsuccessful teacher" who cannot control her pupils (117).

His behavior seems rude and grating, but Frances is not insulted, because she perceives his interest in her beneath his imperious façade. His courtship of Frances is almost funny, because he can only make them both at ease by emphasizing the teacher/pupil relationship between them, by demanding that Frances read English to him. By the end of the novel, however, he is using his imperious professorial style only to raise a sparkle of defiance in Frances, which he finds thrilling because he can quickly quell her back into submission.

Like his friend Hunsden, William seems to despise those more powerful than himself and to seek out those less powerful. He is attracted to Frances Henri's despondent attitude and to her "penniless and parentless" state in the world (138). She is even worse off than he, so he can confer on her the gift of his affection and have it appreciated. On the other hand, he feels threatened by his uncles, his brother, Hunsden, Zoraïde, and Pelet. All of these characters attempt to manipulate and control him, instead of treating him as an equal. The only person of higher social status who makes him comfortable is M. Vandenhuten, the wealthy father of one of his students who had helped him find a position after he left M. Pelet's establishment. William is at ease because both he and Vandenhuten seem to acknowledge the superiority of William's mind, which has "more fire and action" than the Dutchman's (174). William is gratified to think of himself as Frances's "master" and to have her call him "mon maître." After their marriage, William exults in the fact that Frances is always respectful, deferent, and "as docile as a well-trained child" (205). Although both spouses work full time, Frances reverts back from schoolmistress to "my own little lace-mender" at home, and at her school "it was her pleasure, her joy to make me still the master in all things" (209).

William can finally relax his vigilant self-control after attaining the social and financial position appropriate to his talents and education. He has become more self-confident, since he has resisted temptations, overcome obstacles, and proven his philosophy of life—that hope really does smile on effort. Rather than being mastered, he has become a master, his rightful place in Charlotte Brontë's universe.

Edward Crimsworth is William's first contestant in the battle for dominance. Edward does not have an aristocrat's education, but he is healthy, strong, vigorous, determined, and ruthless. "As an animal," William notes, "Edward excelled me far; should he prove as paramount in mind as in person I must be his slave" (10). Ten years older than William, Edward hates the aristocracy and everything connected to it, because his wealthy aristocratic uncles refused to help their destitute, pregnant, and dying sister (Edward and William's mother) even after her husband's death. He despises a liberal arts education as worthless trash, and he never attends church because he "owned no God but Mammon" (14). Edward may even blame William for their mother's death, as he seems to have offered William a job only to humiliate and destroy him. Edward's prejudice against aristocrats makes him think this will be easy, so when his genteelly raised brother displays the good work habits of the rising middle classes, instead of the dissolute, idle, and spendthrift ways he was expecting to see in one so educated, Edward is outraged. Finding his brother cool and apparently unperturbed by being treated as a mere employee, Edward becomes even more determined to break William's spirit.

When Edward threatens to horsewhip William, William grabs the whip, breaks it in half, and walks out the door the winner in this battle of wills. William has proven his superiority, which is the result of his education, intelligence, and self-control. Edward continues to tyrannize his employees, and when his factory fails he also tyrannizes his wife to the point where she leaves him and returns to her family. However, characters like Edward cannot be kept down. He is soon back in business again, and he persuades his wife to return to him. Although Edward may always be wealthier and more powerful than William, his lack of education, manners, and self-control allow William to feel superior to his brother.

Yorke Hunsden does business with Edward in the wool manufacturing industry. Rather than being a self-made man, however, he is the descendant of an old and respected family, who own a large estate and have been independent for centuries. Hunsden has gone into business only to restore the family fortune, so that he can live independently again—that is to say, without working. Hunsden is remarkably similar to Charles, the old school friend William writes to at the beginning of the novel, who was "sarcastic, observant, shrewd, cold-blooded" and who always checked any flights of romantic fancy with "sardonic coldness" (1). There was an "animal attraction" between William and Charles, an attraction between two personalities who delighted in dueling with their intellects and scorning each other's opinions. Hunsden feels the same kind of attraction to William Crimsworth. But the friendship between Hunsden and William, like that between William and Charles, is not close and mutually supportive. Hunsden delights in trying to unnerve Crimsworth, and Crimsworth delights in maintaining his composure despite all the insults Hunsden can hurl at him.

Like Hiram Yorke in *Shirley*, Hunsden claims to be a democrat and a radical reformer simply because he hates to have people above him in rank and social standing. He despises the aristocracy yet takes pride in his own family name and heritage. Despite his democratic principles, he would never consider marrying below his social position, and he is at first appalled that Crimsworth is marrying a lace mender. Hunsden descends from the Saxons, who were defeated by the Normans in 1066 in what is known as the Norman Conquest of England. Since aristocratic titles descend from these Norman conquerors,

Hunsden scorns and resents them. He feels as proud of his heritage as "any peer in the realm of his Norman race and Conquest-dated title" (192), and he will never doubt his own superiority to just about everyone.

Only a few years older than Crimsworth, Hunsden is nevertheless a man of the world. He has traveled abroad and gained a brusque and forward self-confidence that is often offensive. He claims to despise William's aristocratic features and manner, while admiring Edward's physique, strength, and pride in a mercantile heritage. However, Hunsden has many more aristocratic than bourgeois traits. He is not strongly built, he is educated and cultured, and he will inherit a large estate.

Hunsden despises Edward's treatment of William because the former was violating the latter's "natural claim to equality" (37). Because he will always resist a tyrant, Hunsden gets William fired to free him from bondage. But the man who despises "dirty bread" can hardly believe that William has severed relations with his rich uncles for idealistic reasons alone (37–39).

Besides being a hypocrite, Hunsden is sexually ambiguous. His face, figure, and handwriting are neither masculine nor feminine. Crimsworth may suspect that he is a homosexual, as when he comments on Hunsden's sexually ambiguous handwriting being indicative of "certain traits I suspected, rather than knew, to appertain to his nature" (159). He may represent the threat of homosexuality to Crimsworth, who certainly feels threatened and intimidated by Hunsden's brashness and bold commentary on Crimsworth's faults. Once engaged to Frances, Crimsworth finally shakes off the threat Hunsden poses during a highly suggestive physical fight: "He swayed me to and fro; so I grappled him round the waist . . . we had then a tug for it" (201).

Hunsden is usually alone or in the company of other men, and although he at times expresses the desire to find the perfect woman to be his wife, his standards are so high that he will never find her. He falls in love with a fierce and beautiful actress, but he refuses to marry below his social class, and never considers marrying any of the socially acceptable young ladies in his neighborhood. For William, Hunsden's sexual ambiguity represents the threat of sexual indulgence or sensuality outside the boundaries of morality. Once William is married, he is safe from being seduced by Hunsden's lifestyle.

However, Hunsden presents other threats to William as well. He "had learnt somewhere, somehow, the art of setting himself quite at his ease, and of allowing no insular timidity to intervene as a barrier between him and his convenience or pleasure" (20). William cannot afford to follow this example, and he makes sure his desires are always controlled by reason. Hunsden thinks the passionate spirit should be given free rein and does not think Victor, Crimsworth's son, should be sent to school. An English school would instill in Victor the kind of steely self-control that Hunsden scorns, but that William thinks is necessary to curb Victor's spirit (221).

Hunsden doesn't change or develop as a character, but the friendship between Hunsden and William becomes less antagonistic after William's marriage. When William becomes Hunsden's neighbor in England, they maintain a cordial but somewhat distant relationship. With his house full of guests from all over the world, Hunsden brings an occasional taste of the outside world to William and Frances, who would otherwise live completely absorbed in marital harmony, isolated from all the world. Hunsden's worldliness is contrasted with the idealized relationship between Frances and Crimsworth.

Although no longer a threat to William, Hunsden does however begin to present a threat to Victor, William's son. Victor is extremely fond of Hunsden, and the two spend considerable time together, but both Frances and William are anxious about their relationship. Both parents worry when they see Hunsden and Victor seated together that Hunsden is "instilling God knows what principles into his ear" (221). Frances even "roves with restless movement round, like a dove guarding its young from a hovering hawk" (221). Hunsden is like a hawk threatening to pluck Victor out of the nest by instilling Victor with ideas and values that are antithetical to Crimsworth's.

Victor has received a mastiff pup from Hunsden, which Victor adores and even calls Yorke. The novel ends with the startling scene of Crimsworth shooting Yorke right in the front yard of his home, in his son's view. Yorke is killed at the same time both parents have decided to send Victor to Eton, despite Hunsden's disapproval. Hunsden's values have been soundly rejected by the Crimsworths, a move symbolized by the dog's death.

M. François Pelet, William's first employer in Brussels, also represents a way of life William must reject. The director of a successful boys' school, Pelet is presented as the opposite of Edward, William's brother. While Edward is fierce and threatening, Pelet is quiet, mild, and pensive. Yet Pelet controls his boys with a quiet glance more effectively than Edward succeeds in controlling his employees with shouting and threats. William admires Pelet's quiet power, his ability to hide his true nature from others, and his perfect manners.

However, when Pelet does reveal his true nature, William no longer admires him. Pelet avoids the subject of women because he realizes that coarse talk and references to his past sexual conquests offend Crimsworth. Pelet sees that Crimsworth is an idealist when it comes to women, and he decides to test his fiancée's fidelity by having Crimsworth believe she is unattached. Knowing that Zoraïde loves to make a conquest of every man and that he is not precisely the physical type of man Zoraïde admires, Pelet is motivated by insecurity and jealousy. Pelet thinks he has found Crimsworth's weak spot, but Crimsworth has found an even greater weakness in the otherwise perfectly controlled schoolmaster. Pelet reveals just how jealous and insecure he is one night when he arrives home completely drunk, ranting and raving about wanting to kill Crimsworth, who ends up putting the out-of-control Pelet to bed.

Pelet never knows that Crimsworth has witnessed his mad ranting, since he can't remember anything that happened, but Crimsworth continues to scorn Pelet and keep him at a formal distance. After Zoraïde convinces Pelet that she has never had any interest in Crimsworth, the two are soon married. Pelet is blinded by his passion, and, it is suggested, he becomes the type of husband he had previously scorned—the unsuspecting husband of an unfaithful wife. Zoraïde and Pelet's marriage does not include the domestic harmony that William values, even though their two schools become even more profitable and respected.

Zoraïde Reuter, the director of the "Pensionnat de Demoiselles" adjacent to M. Pelet's boys' boarding school, is about thirty years old when Crimsworth first meets her. Crimsworth immediately admires her grace, exquisite manners, and calm, unflappable exterior. Like William and Pelet, Zoraïde is unusually capable of hiding her true nature. Beneath her graceful and calm exterior, however, she harbors a suspicious, sly, crafty, and dissembling nature. She is skilled in the art of observing without being observed, a quality Crimsworth also admires and displays. Crimsworth begins to fall in love with her, but after discovering that she is engaged to Pelet, he positively scorns her.

Zoraïde has good sense and amazing self-control, so it is strange that she would fall in love with a young, poor teacher like Crimsworth. However, her debased and perverted nature causes her to pursue an immoral desire without restraint. She uses audacious flattery to win Crimsworth's esteem, and she treats him like "the great Mogul," offering him numerous little services. She is a woman who always tramples on the humble and honest but is fascinated by pride, haughtiness, selfishness, and tyranny. Since Crimsworth is purposefully displaying these negative qualities, she cannot resist him. He feels that she brings out all that is evil and immoral in his nature. The qualities she values most in others are not Crimsworth's values, but she seems to infer that he possesses these qualities because of his stern indifference to her every charm and blandishment.

Zoraïde seems fascinated by Crimsworth precisely because she cannot get him under her power as she has done her other professors. It is his resignation from her establishment that promptly snaps her back to her senses. She becomes practical and mercenary again, quickly patching up her relationship with Pelet. Even though she does not love him, he is wealthy, convenient, and in love with her. Crimsworth abhors this type of marriage, made for money and position alone. Like Hunsden, Zoraïde is a trap that William must avoid. She represents sensual pleasure, which Crimsworth feels is sinful if not associated with true love and respect, whether or not the parties are married to each other.

Frances Henri is an immigrant from Switzerland, an orphan who has long been living with her aunt. She teaches lace mending at Mademoiselle Reuter's Pensionnat and has asked to sit in on Crimsworth's English classes, because her mother was an Englishwoman. She had known how to speak English when she had someone with whom to speak it but has now forgotten it. For Crimsworth, she stands out because she has a purer English accent and can write with imagination and expression in the English language. However, while these academic qualities may have attracted Crimsworth's notice, he is even more impressed by her character. She has a sense of duty and an ability to persevere not evidenced in the other students. Her practical, humble, and dutiful nature is evidenced by her begging her aunt to have her taught the trade of lace mending as soon as they arrived in Brussels, because she can learn it in a few days and find immediate employment.

Because lace mending is a despised, poorly paid trade, Frances is not respected by her students. They take advantage of her because she is depressed and easily hurt. Being singled out by Crimsworth, however, gives Frances inner strength. She begins to blossom as her gifts are recognized, and she regains her inner strength to struggle against adversity. However, Zoraïde, jealous of the attention Crimsworth pays to her, fires her, refuses to let her back in the door of the school so that she can say good-bye to Crimsworth, and refuses to give Crimsworth her address. When Crimsworth finds her at the Protestant cemetery, they bring each other back to life from the brink of a deathlike despair. Like Crimsworth, she is skilled in "self-denial and self-control" (138), in keeping passion under the control of reason, because she also has had to make her own way in the world. But with Crimsworth she is not on the defensive. She allows Crimsworth to hold her spellbound and to "rule her" completely (164), because she trusts him not to harm her. Only to him does she reveal the intelligence and fire of her true nature, which she has hidden from the rest of the world because they are not consistent with her social standing. Crimsworth similarly reveals his true nature to her, but not until he becomes sure of her love by reading her long poem (183).

Even before they marry, however, Frances begins to reveal her strength, determination, and ambition. She will not marry Crimsworth if he will not allow her to keep her teaching position, even though her salary is much smaller than his. She plans not only to work, but also to advance in her profession. After they have been married for some years, she decides that she is not being fairly compensated and opens her own school. She even insists that her husband visit her school every day and teach a lesson there, so that he will know what *she* has been doing all day and be able to converse about it.

Once happily married and in a position of financial stability, Frances can finally utilize her innate abilities. She becomes an excellent, spirited, engaging teacher and a competent, loved, and respected administrator. With her husband, however, Frances becomes a demure, deferential, and respectful wife. She is capable of spirited debates, as shown by her argument about patriotism with Hunsden, but she would never challenge her own husband so blatantly. With him she wins her point through feminine charms rather than masculine aggression, and she never fails to show a "gentle homage" to her master (210).

Even after Victor is born, Frances continues to work, which was rare among women of her economic and social position. Meaningful work and a change in the marriage laws of England were on the minds of many women in the mid-nineteenth century, and through Frances, Charlotte addresses both issues. When William asks her what she would do if married to a brute, she said she would run away if he could not be reformed.

Her keen intelligence is displayed when she accurately analyzes the reasons Hunsden cannot marry his ideal woman Lucia, although she never speaks this way to William. Her strength of character is shown when she doesn't argue for keeping Victor longer at home, for she is even more determined than her husband to go through the painful separation of sending her only child off to school, because she believes it is best for his future. Frances blossoms into an effective teacher, a competent administrator, and a good mother. The emotional and financial security provided by her marriage to a supportive husband have allowed her to develop and utilize her innate talents and abilities.

THEMATIC ISSUES

In her 1856 preface to *The Professor*, Charlotte Brontë expressly states her thematic purposes. She wanted to write a very realistic novel in which her hero would work his way up in life instead of marrying an heiress or inheriting an unexpected fortune. As most men do, he would have ups and downs, but he would experience no fantastic successes nor gross failures. Having the novel rejected by many publishers, Charlotte had come to the conclusion that real life realistically portrayed did not make popular fiction. Readers and publishers wanted the fantastic, the romantic, the unexpected fortune, the raging tyrant, and the passionate lover. Charlotte's didactic purpose in writing the novel was to show that hard work, combined with the proper lifestyle, could lead to success in life.

Hard work and clean living require self-control, which is another important theme in the novel. England was a stratified class society where one's inherited title, name, and wealth had been the only factors that influenced one's social standing, but the nineteenth-century self-improvement movement claimed that upward mobility was possible, if one had innate intelligence, character, and ability as well as perseverance and self-control. William shows his self-control by not allowing himself to show anger at his brother, by resisting his students' coquetry, and by resisting Zoraïde's attempted seduction.

Domination is another theme in the novel, and self-control is one way to gain power over others while resisting their having power over you. Another is the ability to read your opponent's character and motives without revealing your own. Crimsworth is vulnerable as a young man starting to make his way in the world, so he makes sure that his face and voice never reveal his true thoughts in order that others do not find his weak points and take advantage of them. With Edward, Crimsworth fights a mental duel to see whose personality will prevail. William wins this first battle because he can see his brother's weak points and use them to his advantage, while Edward can find no chink in William's armor.

Zoraïde Reuter attempts to find Crimsworth's weak point so that she can control him. At first this is strictly a business maneuver, but as soon as Crimsworth seems invincible, Zoraïde becomes ensnared in her own trap of trying to find his vulnerabilities. She reveals her own weak point—she cannot bear to be neither loved, admired, nor feared.

In order to safeguard the self, the mask one shows to the world is only removed in private, among those one loves and trusts. Unlike Crimsworth, Frances Henri is an open book. All are able to read her vulnerable points, and her pupils take advantage of her mercilessly until Crimsworth gives her the strength to become invulnerable to their jibes. Frances learns how to face the world with complete self-control, once she has the strength and energy. To Crimsworth, however, Frances continues to reveal her true personality, because she loves and trusts him.

The battle for social advancement is another important theme, and a character's mind and soul are his weapons—more than money, social class, or physical strength. As in all battles, it is best to keep one's weapons hidden until they are needed so that they will work more effectively during the surprise attack. Crimsworth admires the way Pelet hides his true nature, and he is sure that there is "flint or steel under an external covering of velvet" (54). However, too much self-control can turn a person into a statue. Old maids who have lived with "resignation and endurance" their entire lives eventually lose the capacity to love or to express their inner nature, and they die mere husks of human beings, with hearts long withered and dried in their bosoms (179). The object of self-control and self-concealment is social advancement, but one must also find a true friend to whom one can finally reveal the long-hidden inner self. With Frances, "Reason," which has long counseled Crimsworth to wear his impenetrable mask, finally steps aside and allows "Instinct" to act (184).

Part of Crimsworth's vulnerability is his lack of a secure masculine identity. Crimsworth must fiercely oppose those who wish to dominate him—his brother, Yorke Hunsden, Pelet, and Zoraïde Reuter—in order to establish his own masculinity. Then he must find a feminine creature whom he himself can dominate, if he wishes to be securely male. William finds in Frances a woman with spirit and intelligence who nevertheless loves to be subservient to her master, Crimsworth. He can love her unreservedly because she does not threaten him or try to outmaneuver him.

Another theme of the novel is the true nature of young women, or what they hide behind their social masks. His female students do not bother hiding their vices and faults from Crimsworth, who spends many pages painting unflattering portraits of them. The purpose of self-control and self-concealment is to gain a better place in the world, and these girls sincerely doubt that their English professor will in any way influence their future. Crimsworth therefore sees a side of these young women rarely shown to the male sex—dishonesty, dirtiness, audacious and coquettish manners, foul language, angry, sullen faces, and dull intellects.

While these girls may see marriage as their ticket to security and social status, Crimsworth can gain security and status only by gaining his liberty. "I must follow my own devices—I must till the day of my death; because I can neither comprehend, adopt, nor work out those of other people" (39), William tells Hunsden after quitting his job at his brother's mill. Frances is similarly oppressed by working for others, but she is wonderfully effective when running her own school. William and Frances believe that people of similar intellects and abilities have a "natural claim to equality"(37) despite any differences in wealth, social class, appearance, or gender. Hunsden mouths this philosophy of equality, but he rarely acts on it. Charlotte Brontë's position as a poor but educated woman of genius, whose father had recently risen from the peasantry of Ireland, made her very conscious of the difficulty of claiming her equality, not to mention her superiority, before the world.

HISTORICAL/SOCIAL-CULTURAL CONTEXTS

The Professor takes place in the same location and historical period as does *Villette*, so the historical and cultural contexts are very similar. Besides denouncing Catholicism, commenting on the status of women, and using phrenology as a device to reveal character, Charlotte uses stereotypical ethnic characteristics, nineteenth-century psychology, and references to the great debate between idealism (or romanticism) and materialism (or pragmatism).

Belgium has been, since its birth as a nation in 1830, a multicultural, half French and half Flemish (Dutch) nation, with a tiny German population. The

French had almost complete control of the government and the professions during the first century of Belgium's existence, discriminating against the Flamands. Both Crimsworth and Pelet feel justified in discriminating against the Flemish, claiming they are stupid and sluggish. Although Zoraïde Reuter is Belgian, we assume that she is French Belgian and not Flemish Belgian, since both she and her mother always speak French.

Crimsworth describes his students at the boys' school as "intellectually weak," stubborn, lazy, dense, but collectively rebellious if pushed an inch beyond their limits. He attributes their character traits to their being Flemish, as if the physical land that gave them birth (flat, boring, fertile) also gave them their characters. This belief in inherited moral and intellectual characteristics is also reflected in the many references to phrenology, the "science" of reading a person's character by the shape or "bumps" on their skull that was discussed in Chapter 3.

Phrenology and inherited characteristics seem to contradict the Victorian ideology of self-help and the entire theme of the novel, that hope smiles on effort and that hard work leads to success. But many phrenologists and other self-help experts claimed that with enough effort it was possible to develop the good traits and extinguish or minimize the bad traits. The shape of the head revealed the natural tendencies of moral and intellectual character, but these tendencies could be developed or repressed. This philosophy allowed for the possibility of rising in social status through self-control and diligence. It is also important to note that Charlotte's heroes and heroines never raise themselves out of ten generations of ignorance and poverty. Crimsworth's mother was an aristocrat and his father a successful businessman; therefore he has inherited talent, intelligence, and sensitivity, which will make it possible for him to attain his rightful place in the social order. It may not be apparent to others, but Crimsworth knows that his rightful place is as master, not mastered, and he will settle for nothing less.

Brontë also touches on the relatively new science of psychology when she describes William's hypochondria (190). Hypochondria referred to an illness with mental rather than physical symptoms, usually extreme depression. Physicians were sure that hypochondria, or what we would today call major depression, had an unknown physical, as opposed to a psychological, cause. Charlotte Brontë experienced many episodes of severe depression, and most of her main characters also battle this demon. The cause of Crimsworth's first bout with hypochondria, which lasted an entire year, could describe the causes of Charlotte's own depression: "Finding me lost in vague mental wanderings, with many affections and few objects, glowing aspirations and gloomy prospects, strong desires and slender hopes" (190), the sorceress hypochondria lures the young Crimsworth into a longing for death. William's second bout of hypochondria occurs just after he has proposed to and been accepted by Frances, which is the happiest moment of his life. He has, however, endured great stresses, and he is just about to start creating a family, and family life is something he himself has missed. Thoughts of family may lead to thoughts of death, and William, like all of Charlotte's heroines, has to decide, as Robert Keefe points out, if it is better to live or to die. William chooses to live.

Charlotte Brontë also represents the two sides of a very important nineteenth-century debate by using Hunsden and Frances as spokespersons. Hunsden claims to be a materialist. He denies that the English are any more intelligent or moral than other nationalities. He claims they are respected only because they have wealth. He denies the existence of anything like patriotism or spirituality that cannot be weighed and measured. He represents Jeremy Bentham's (1748–1832) view that man is motivated only by self-interest, that whatever increases pleasure and reduces pain is good, and that whatever produces the greatest happiness for the greatest number of people is by definition the greatest good. Frances Henri, on the other hand, is an idealist. She believes that patriotism and love are just as real as money and land. Both she and William are often motivated by what appear to be idealistic feelings. Frances cares for her sick aunt even though she may suspect that she will lose her job as a result. William quits his position at Pelet's against the dictates of common sense and the greatest immediate good for the greatest number of people. Simply to avoid the temptation of adultery, William impoverishes himself and makes it impossible for him to propose to Frances, to say nothing of denying Pelet his services as a teacher and Zoraïde a pleasant distraction. To the idealist, there is a greater good than material welfare. One's spiritual welfare is even more important.

Materialists also think little of the imagination, because it is unquantifiable, and of abstractions like patriotism and nationalism, because these ideas are often the glue that holds unjust social systems together. Frances and William are romantics, since they believe that imagination makes the world human and beautiful. Frances tells Hunsden, "Your method is to squeeze the sap out of creation and make manure of the refuse, by way of turning it to what you call use" (198).

The role of married women is also an important issue in *The Professor*, as it is in all of Charlotte's novels. As in *Villette*, the narrator thinks little of "the idea of marrying a doll or a fool" (87), but here the narrator is a man, not a despairing disillusioned Lucy Snowe comparing herself to Polly Home. Charlotte presents her ideal of a perfect marriage as a partnership between like-minded persons who not only love but also respect each other, and who work together. Crimsworth wants a wife he can talk to about his intellectual interests. He is not impressed by his brother's wife, even though she is beautiful, lively, and charming, because she seems childish and ignorant. Because he is a teacher,

Crimsworth is attracted to the intelligent, creative, industrious Frances, who will make him a much better wife than could any woman who captivated him based on her beauty and charm alone. As a good husband, Crimsworth allows Frances to be a working wife and then a working mother, completely supporting her while she sets up and runs her school.

LITERARY DEVICES AND CRAFT

The first literary device to become apparent is the use of a first-person narrator. The novel opens as William's letter to Charles, a friend from Eton, but by the end of the first chapter Brontë has Crimsworth abandon the pretense of writing a letter and decide to continue his story as a narrative for a wider audience. The first-person narrator is also male, while the author is female, and some readers may feel that the author is unsuccessful in portraying the inner life of a man. Crimsworth always seems stuffy and stilted, like a walking stick passing through life rather than a man.

The first-person narrative is also complicated by the fact that many autobiographical experiences from the author's own life are included as Crimsworth's recollections, even though these memories are sometimes irrelevant and sometimes not in character with the narrator's past experiences as we know them. The entire affair between Crimsworth, Zoraïde, and Frances is a rewriting of Charlotte's experiences in Brussels with M. Heger and his wife Zoë. But some of Charlotte's own experiences that had nothing to do with Belgium are also included. For example, at the beginning of Chapter 19, the narrator first offers a prescription for novelists and then a description of a soul degraded by vice, which sounds like a description of Charlotte's brother Branwell's descent into alcoholism and drug addiction. Similarly, Crimsworth decides to move out of Pelet's house because he has previously witnessed the terrible effects of adultery, but what is described is Branwell's descent into madness after being fired for having an affair with his employer's wife. Branwell was convinced that the lady would seek him out after her husband's death, but when she shunned him instead, Branwell lost himself in self-pity, aggravating his addiction to alcohol and opium.

Autobiography and fiction again meld when Crimsworth reads Frances's poem. We are treated to a double reflection when Crimsworth says that the poem was "not exactly the writer's own experience" but composed of scenes that experience suggested, thereby avoiding egotism, exercising the imagination, and soothing the heart (180). The poem, which was written earlier than the novel, refers to Charlotte's love for M. Heger as well as to Frances's love for Crimsworth. Like the poem, *The Professor* has a happy ending; the poem reflects the novel, while the novel, in turn, reflects the life of the author in a series of ever-receding mirrors.

Another important literary device is metaphor and imagery, as when Crimsworth "buckled on a breast-plate of steely indifference, and let down a visor of impassible austerity" (68) so that he could look at the sensuous, seductive, impudently flirtatious girls in his class without being harmed. This image of Crimsworth as a knight, lowering his visor to battle a hoard of harpies, highlights the allusions to the knights in Spenser's *The Faerie Queene* (published between 1589 and 1596), who must battle with and defeat (among other things) various female personifications of evil. Crimsworth's students "launch" at him various looks that he describes as "artillery" (79). He is able to overcome "the enchantment, the golden haze" of his adversaries, the schoolgirls (69), just as Greek heroes must escape female enchantresses such as Circe, who lured men to her island and then turned them into swine. He even describes one of his pupils as "Gorgon-like" (79). He must avoid gazing at her directly and only look at her through the reflection in his armor, in order to avoid being turned to stone.

The imagery is of course replete with allusions to Greek myths, the Bible, and the classics of English literature. These allusions are a third important literary device. For example, when Crimsworth writes to his friend Charles that their friendship was not of the "Pylades and Orestes" type, he refers to the Greek myth in which Pylades is such a good friend to Orestes that he willingly helps the latter stab his mother Clytemnestra to death, and he then willingly accompanies Orestes though every punishment meted out to him by the gods. While the relationship between Pylades and Orestes was not overtly homosexual, Hunsden's allusions to the Bible can be more easily interpreted as a homosexual threat. When he catches Crimsworth racing home from work he says, "Just so must Lot have left Sodom" (23) and in the next breath he says he must be content with Crimsworth since God has not sent him Rebecca on a camel's hump. Crimsworth is trying to escape domination by other men. He escapes from his brother's tyranny only to find himself being harangued by Hunsden. These are only a few of the allusions in *The Professor* that can add another level of meaning to our understanding of the text.

Personification is another important literary device. As in her other novels, Brontë personifies the various elements of the psyche that are in mental warfare with each other. Reason battles with passion, as when Crimsworth does not allow himself to kiss Frances good-bye (45). Similarly, the "Spirit of Evil" wrestles with the "Deity of Love" for Crimsworth's soul when he wonders if he should resign his position at Pelet's. Crimsworth resists "Temptation" and turns in his resignation (155).

Obviously symbolic dreams are another literary device Brontë uses here and in all her novels. Crimsworth dreams of a rainbow in a bank of clouds, and he sees an angel pointing to the rainbow, which he interprets as a sign that "Hope smiles on Effort" (147). The dream is telling him not to despair because he has resigned his position at Pelet's and therefore hasn't the means to support Frances as his wife. These symbolic dreams often mark major turning points in Charlotte's novels.

ALTERNATIVE PERSPECTIVE: POSTCOLONIAL CRITICISM

Postcolonial literary criticism, also called multicultural literary criticism, includes several approaches to literature. One branch seeks to show how great works of literature by non-Western and nonwhite authors have been denied a place in the literary canon, which is that group of works regarded as representing the best that have been written and most worthy of being taught. Until recently the literary canon was composed almost exclusively of works written by white Western European men. Feminist critics have worked hard to include more works by women in the canon, while postcolonial critics have worked tirelessly to have literature by African, Asian, and African American authors included.

Another branch of postcolonial criticism seeks to show how canonical literature is itself a tool of domination. It spreads and reinforces the racism and imperialism of colonizing and dominating nations such as England, France, and the United States. Postcolonial literary theorist Edward Said's *Orientalism* (1978), sometimes considered the founding text of postcolonial studies, argues that Western literature represents non-Westerners and nonwhites in negatively stereotypical ways. They are represented as lazy, dishonest, sexually promiscuous, irrational, irresponsible, ignorant, and further down the scale of human development. When readers from dominant cultures read this literature, they find it easy to justify domination and even destruction of other less powerful cultures. Readers from the dominated or colonized cultures, who are often forced to read these Western texts in Western-style schools, learn to despise themselves and their culture and to identify with the powerful colonizers. Language itself is used as a tool of domination when marginalized peoples are forced to learn and speak the language of the colonizer and reprimanded for speaking their native tongue or dialect.

Teaching the English language to a "lesser" culture and ethnic group is the subject of *The Professor*. Without even touching on the assumed superiority of whites over nonwhites or Western European culture over non-Western cultures, Brontë manages to display all the faults of the colonial writer who justifies British imperialism. As a woman, Brontë is part of a marginalized group, a fact that she recognizes and confronts in *The Professor* as well as in her other novels. As a nineteenth-century Englishwoman, however, Brontë belonged to the most powerful nation on earth, with an ever expanding colonial empire spanning the entire globe, and Brontë wholeheartedly reinforces the idea that the British are a superior "race" or ethnic group.

Crimsworth is a poor, despised counting-house clerk in England, but as a schoolteacher in Brussels he soon begins to feel powerful and superior. He immediately feels more self-confident and more intelligent, because he sees in the Flemish faces around him "intellectual inferiority . . . in lines none can mistake" (54).

Teaching English makes Crimsworth feel superior and powerful, since it is the language of culture and intellect. He describes his male Belgian students as having "short memories, dense intelligence, [and] feeble reflective powers" (52). They are like cattle who must be prodded along at a slow pace. If one asked too much of them, they would revolt like "desperate swine" (52). Using animal imagery to describe the members of other cultures is a common method of dehumanizing them. Crimsworth believes the history of the Belgian nation (its having been occupied or overrun by different conquerors for centuries) is proof that the Flemish are slow, stupid, and cowardly, the products of a land where "the climate is such as to induce degeneracy of the human mind and body" (80).

The idea of "the other" is central in postcolonial studies. A group, class, or nation can only define itself against what it is not. Frantz Fanon (1925–1961), a central figure in postcolonial studies and author of two highly influential books—*Black Skin, White Masks* (1952) and *The Wretched of the Earth* (1961)—shows how the category "white" cannot exist without the category "black." Similarly, the category "British" cannot exist without the category "Non-British." This explains why Crimsworth, who is despised and oppressed in England, must leave England to become successful. His "Englishness" carries no weight in England itself, where this category is subdivided into patrician and plebian, aristocracy and working class, rich and poor, southern and northern, educated and uneducated. In Belgium, however, his English birth suddenly has value, because it is perceived by himself and many others as superior to being Belgian, especially. In addition, the English language suddenly becomes valuable as a commodity to be sold. As a great colonial power, England exports its language and culture throughout the world. Crimsworth advances in the world by teaching English in Belgium, but one could not advance in England by teaching Flemish, since that culture is considered insignificant.

Fanon discusses how language is used as a weapon of colonization. The language of the powerful colonizer becomes valuable as a tool of survival and advancement for the colonized. The native language, which contains within it the indigenous way of knowing and the cultural history of the race, is devalued and sometimes even forgotten. In Belgium, the French imposed their language on the Flemish, since all government business and professional work was conducted in French alone. The Flemish battle for equality in Belgium has been a battle for the supremacy of their language over the French language in those provinces that are primarily Flemish. Brontë's hierarchy of cultural worth is clearly apparent. The British are unquestionably superior, the French are culturally advanced but morally corrupt, and the Flemish are stupid and slow. Crimsworth battles for the supremacy of English over French by constantly badgering Frances to speak English, even after they are married. Crimsworth notices Frances because she has a good English accent. He therefore thinks her essays may reveal a higher level of intelligence and sensitivity, which they do. Her genetic heritage is superior to that of her classmates, because her mother was British, but she must still master the English language as part of her intellectual and artistic development.

Increased interest in ethnic identity and cultural tradition in England itself is evidenced by Hunsden's pride in his Saxon heritage, and his disdain of the Norman conquerors with their kings and aristocratic titles. This emphasis on ethnic identity influenced the rise of nationalism in Europe. Many critics have noted Brontë's imperialism and negative representations of people from other cultures and social classes, and they have related it to the rising tide of nationalism during the period of Britain's rapid colonial expansion.

Bibliography

WORKS BY CHARLOTTE AND EMILY BRONTË

Note: Many editions of the Brontë novels have been published and several are still in publication. I have chosen to use currently available paperback editions often used in classrooms. Page numbers referred to in the text are to the editions of the novels listed below.

Brontë, Charlotte. *The Complete Poems of Charlotte Brontë*. Ed. Clement Shorter and C. W. Hatfield. London: Hodder and Stoughton, 1923.

———. *An Edition of the Early Writings of Charlotte Brontë*. 2 vol. Ed. Christine Alexander. Oxford, UK, and New York: Shakespeare Head (Blackwell), 1987.

———. *Five Novelettes, Transcribed from the Original Manuscripts*. Ed. Winifred Gérin. London: Folio Society, 1971.

———. *Jane Eyre*. 1847. Ed. Richard J. Dunn. 2nd ed. New York: Norton, 1987.

———. *Letters of Charlotte Brontë*. Vol. I. Ed. Margaret Smith and Judith Hattaway. Oxford: Clarendon, 1995– . (Three volumes are anticipated).

———. *The Professor*. 1857. London: J. M. Dent & Sons, 1985.

———. *Shirley*. 1849. Ed. Andrew and Judith Hook. London: Penguin, 1985.

———. *Villette*. 1853. Ed. Mark Lilly. New York: Penguin, 1979.

Brontë, Charlotte, and Emily Brontë. *The Belgian Essays*. Ed. and trans. Sue Lanoff. New Haven: Yale University Press, 1996.

———. *The Shakespeare Head Brontë*. 19 vols. Ed. T. J. Wise and J. A. Symington. Oxford: Shakespeare Head, 1931–1938.

Brontë, Emily. *The Complete Poems of Emily Jane Brontë*. Ed. Philip Henderson. London: Folio Society, 1951.

———. *The Poems of Emily Brontë*. Ed. Derek Roper. Oxford: Clarendon, 1995.

———. *Wuthering Heights*. 1847. Ed. William M. Sale, Jr., and Richard J. Dunn. New York: Norton, 1990.

BIOGRAPHIES

Barker, Juliet. *The Brontës*. London: Weidenfeld and Nicholson, 1994.

———. *The Brontës: A Life in Letters*. Woodstock: Overlook, 1998.

Chitham, Edward. *A Life of Emily Brontë*. London: Basil Blackwell, 1987.

Frank, Katherine. *Emily Brontë: A Chainless Soul*. Boston: Houghton Mifflin, 1990.

Fraser, Rebecca. *The Brontës: Charlotte Brontë and Her Family*. New York: Crown, 1988.

Gaskell, Elizabeth. *The Life of Charlotte Brontë*. 1857. Ed. Alan Shelston. New York: Penguin, 1975.

Gerin, Winifred. *The Brontës*. Ed. Ian Scott-Kilvert. 2 vol. Harlow, England: British Council (Longman Group), 1973–1974.

———. *Charlotte Brontë: The Evolution of Genius*. London: Oxford University Press, 1967.

———. *Emily Brontë: A Biography*. Oxford: Clarendon, 1971.

Gordon, Lyndall. *Charlotte Brontë: A Passionate Life*. London: Chatto & Windus, 1994.

Peters, Margot. *Unquiet Soul: A Biography of Charlotte Brontë*. Garden City, NY: Doubleday, 1975.

Winnifrith, Tom. *A New Life of Charlotte Brontë*. Houndmills, Basingstoke, Hampshire : Macmillan, 1988.

Winnifrith, Tom, and Edward Chitham. *Charlotte and Emily Brontë: Literary Lives*. New York: St. Martin's, 1989.

Wise, T. J., ed. *The Brontës: Their Lives, Friendships and Correspondence*. 2 vols. The Shakespeare Head Press, 1933.

Wise, T. J., and J. A. Symington, eds. *The Shakespeare Head Life and Letters*. 4 vols. Oxford: Shakespeare Head Press, 1932.

JOURNALS DEVOTED TO THE BRONTËS

Brontë Society Transactions: The Journal of Brontë Studies. Ed. Robert Duckett. Published continuously from 1895 to the present. Shipley: Outhwaite Bros.

REVIEWS AND CRITICISM

WUTHERING HEIGHTS

Reviews

Anon. "Wuthering Heights." *Britannia*, January 1848.

Chorley, Henry Fothergill. "*Wuthering Heights.*" *Athenaeum*, December 25, 1847. 1324–1325.

Dobell, Sydney. "Currer Bell." *Palladium.* September 1850.

Lewes, G. H. "Wuthering Heights." *The Leader*, December 28, 1850. 953.

Rigby, Elizabeth. "Wuthering Heights." *Quarterly Review* 84 (1848): 175.

Criticism

Allott, Miriam, ed. *Wuthering Heights, a Casebook.* London: Macmillan, 1992.

Bloom, Harold, ed. *Emily Brontë's Wuthering Heights.* New York: Chelsea House, 1987.

————. *Heathcliff.* New York: Chelsea House, 1992.

Cecil, David. *Early Victorian Novelists.* London: Constable, 1934.

Davies, Stevie. *Emily Brontë: The Artist as a Free Woman.* Manchester: Carcanet Press, 1983.

Gorsky, Susan Rubinov. "'I'll Cry Myself Sick': Illness in *Wuthering Heights.*" *Literature and Medicine* 18:2 (fall 1999): 173–191.

Jacobs, Carol. *Uncontainable Romanticism: Shelley, Brontë, Kleist.* Baltimore: Johns Hopkins University Press, 1989.

Knoepflmacher, U. C. *Wuthering Heights: A Study.* Athens: Ohio University Press, 1994.

Matthews, John T. "Framing in *Wuthering Heights.*" *Wuthering Heights: New Casebooks*, ed. Patsy Stoneman, 54–73. New York: St. Martin's, 1993.

Miles, Peter. *Wuthering Heights: The Critics Debate.* New York: Macmillan, 1990.

Miller, J. Hillis. *The Disappearance of God: Five Nineteenth-Century Writers.* Cambridge: Harvard University Press, 1963.

————. *Fiction and Repetition: Seven English Novels.* Cambridge: Harvard University Press, 1982.

Mitchell, Hayley R., ed. *Readings on Wuthering Heights.* San Diego: Greenhaven, 1999.

Polhemus, Robert M. *Erotic Faith: Being in Love from Jane Austen to D. H. Lawrence.* Chicago: University of Chicago Press, 1990.

Sanger, C. P. "The Structure of *Wuthering Heights.*" *Hogarth Essay* 19 (London: Hogarth, 1926).

Stoneman, Patsy. *Wuthering Heights: New Casebooks.* New York: St. Martin's, 1993.

Van Ghent, Dorothy. *The English Novel: Form and Function.* New York: Holt, Rinehart & Winston, 1953.

Winnifrith, Thomas John, ed. *Critical Essays on Emily Brontë.* New York: G. K. Hall, 1997. 132–143.

JANE EYRE

Reviews

Chorley, Henry Fothergill. "Jane Eyre." *Athenaeum*, October 23, 1847. 1100–1101.

Lewes, G. H. "Recent Novels, French and English." *Frasier's Magazine*, December 1847.

Lewes, G. H. "*Jane Eyre*." *Westminster Review* 48 (1848): 581–584.

Rigby, Elizabeth. "Vanity Fair—and *Jane Eyre*." *Quarterly Review* 84 (December 1848): 173–174.

Criticism

Allott, Miriam. *Charlotte Brontë*: Jane Eyre *and* Villette, *a Casebook*. New York, MacMillan, 1973.

Fraiman, Susan. "Jane Eyre's Fall from Grace." In Jane Eyre: *Case Studies in Contemporary Criticism*, ed. Beth Newman, 614–631. Boston: St. Martin's, 1996.

Hirsch, Marianne. "Jane's Family Romances." In *Borderwork: Feminist Engagements with Comparative Literature*, ed. Margaret R. Higonnet, 162–185. Ithaca: Cornell University Press, 1994.

Hoeveler, Diane Long, and Beth Lau, eds. *Approaches to Teaching Brontë's* Jane Eyre. New York: MLA, 1993.

King, Jeannette. *Jane Eyre*. Philadelphia: Open University Press, 1986.

Lerner, Laurence. "Bertha and the Critics." *Nineteenth-Century Literature* 44:3 (December 1989): 273–300.

Meyer, Susan. "Colonialism and the Figurative Strategy of *Jane Eyre*." In *Macropolitics of Nineteenth-Century Literature: Nationalism, Exoticism, Imperialism*, ed. Jonathan Arac and Harriet Ritvo, 159–183. Philadelphia: University of Pennsylvania Press, 1991.

——— . *Imperialism at Home: Race and Victorian Women's Fiction*. Ithaca, NY: Cornell University Press, 1996.

Millett, Kate. *Sexual Politics*. New York: Doubleday, 1970.

Nestor, Pauline. *Charlotte Brontë's* Jane Eyre. New York: Harvester Wheatsheaf, 1992.

Newman, Beth, ed. *Charlotte Brontë*: Jane Eyre: *Case Studies in Contemporary Criticism*. Boston, MA: Bedford, 1996.

Politi, Jina. "*Jane Eyre* Class-ified." *Literature and History* 8 (1982): 56–66.

Poovy, Mary. "The Anathematized Race: The Governess and Jane Eyre." In *Uneven Developments: The Ideological work of Gender in Mid-Victorian England*, ed. Catherine R. Simpson, 126–163. Chicago: University of Chicago Press, 1988.

Rich, Adrienne. "Jane Eyre: The Temptations of a Motherless Woman." In *On Lies, Secrets and Silence: Selected Prose 1979–1985*. New York: Norton, 1986.

Rose, Karen E. "Fairy-Born and Human-Bred: Jane Eyre's Education in Romance." In *The Voyage In: Fictions of Female Development*, ed. Elizabeth Abel, Marianne Hirsch, and Elizabeth Langland, 69–89. Hanover, NH: University Press of New England, 1983.

Spivak, Gayatri Chakravorty. "Three Women's Texts and a Critique of Imperialism." In *Race, Writing, and Difference*, ed. Henry Louis Gates, Jr., 262–280. Chicago: University of Chicago Press, 1986.

Starks, Lisa S. "Altars to Attics: The Madwoman's Point of View." In *The Aching Hearth: Family Violence in Life and Literature*, ed. Sarah Munson Deats and Lagretta Tallent Lenker, 105–117. New York: Plenum, 1991.

Stockton, Kathryn Bond. *God Between Their Lips: Desire Between Women in Irigaray, Brontë, and Eliot*. Stanford, CA: Stanford University Press, 1994.

Sutherland, John. *Can Jane Eyre Be Happy? More Puzzles in Classic Fiction*. Oxford: Oxford University Press, 1997.

Teachman, Debra. *Understanding* Jane Eyre: *A Student Casebook to Issues, Sources, and Historical Documents*. Westport, CT: Greenwood Press, 2001.

Warhol, Robyn R. "Double Gender, Double Genre in *Jane Eyre* and *Villette*." *SEL: Studies in English Literature, 1500–1900* 36:4 (autumn 1996): 857–875.

Williams, Carolyn. "Closing the Book: The Intertextual End of *Jane Eyre*." In *New Casebooks: Jane Eyre*, ed. Heather Glen. New York: St. Martin's, 1997.

Wyatt, Jean. "A Patriarchy of One's Own: *Jane Eyre* and Romantic Love. *Tulsa Studies in Women's Literature* 4 (1985): 199–216. Reprinted in Barbara Timm Gates, *Critical Essays on Charlotte Brontë*. Boston: G. K. Hall & Co., 1990.

SHIRLEY

Reviews

Chorley, Henry Fothergill. "*Shirley*." *Athenaeum*, November 3, 1849. 1107–1109.

Fonblanque, A. W. Review of *Shirley*. *Examiner*, November 3, 1849.

Lewes, G. H. "*Shirley*." *Edinburgh Review* 91, (1850): 153–173.

Criticism

Argyle, Gisela. "Gender and Generic Mixing in Charlotte Brontë's *Shirley*." *SEL: Studies in English Literature, 1500–1900* 35:4 (fall 1995): 741–756.

Briggs, Asa. "Private and Social Themes in *Shirley*." *Brontë Society Transactions* 13:68 (1958): 203–219.

Hook, Andrew and Judith. "Introduction" *Shirley*, by Charlotte Brontë. New York: Penguin, 1974. 7–32.

Ives, Maura. "Housework, Mill Work, Women's Work: The Functions of Cloth in Charlotte Brontë's *Shirley*." In *Keeping the Victorian House: A Collection of Essays*, ed. Vanessa Dickerson. 259–289. New York: Garland, 1995.

Lashgari, Deirdre. "What Some Women Can't Swallow: Hunger as Protest in Charlotte Brontë's *Shirley*," In *Disorderly Eaters: Texts in Self-Empowerment*, ed. Lilian R. Furst and Peter W. Graham, 141–152. University Park: Pennsylvania State University Press, 1992.

Lawson, Kate. "The Dissenting Voice: *Shirley*'s Vision of Women and Christianity." *Studies in English Literature 1500–1900* 29 (1989): 729–743.

Morris, Pam. "Heroes and Hero-Worship in Charlotte Brontë's *Shirley*." *Nineteenth Century Literature* 54:3 (December 1999).

VILLETTE

Reviews

Chorley, Henry Fothergill. "*Villette*." *Athenaeum*, February 12, 1853. 186–188.

Lewes, H. G. "Villette." *Westminster Review* New Series, vol. 3 (1853): 485–491.

———. "*Villette*." *The Leader*. February 12, 1853.

Martineau, Harriet. "*Villette*." *Daily News*, February 3, 1853.

Criticism

Allott, Miriam. *Charlotte Brontë: Jane Eyre and Villette, a Casebook*. New York, MacMillan, 1973.

Boone, Joseph A. "Depolicing *Villette*." *Novel* 26:1 (fall 1992): 20–42.

Carlisle, Janice. "The Face in the Mirror: *Villette* and the Conventions of Autobiography." *English Literary History* 46 (summer 1979: 262–289). Reprinted in Barbara Timm Gates, *Critical Essays on Charlotte Brontë*. Boston: G. K. Hall, 1990.

Dunbar, Georgia. "Proper Names in *Villette*." *Nineteenth-Century Fiction* 14 (1959–1960): 77–80.

Herrera, Andrea O'Reilly. "'Herself Beheld': Marriage, Motherhood, and Oppression in Brontë's *Villette* and Jacobs's *Incidents in the Life of a Slave Girl*." In *Family Matters in the British and American Novel*, ed. Andrea O'Reilly Herrera, Elizabeth Mahn Nollen, and Sheila Reitzel Foor, 57–77. Bowling Green: Popular Press, 1997.

———. "Imagining a Self Between a Husband or a Wall: Charlotte Brontë's *Villette*." In *The Foreign Woman in British Literature: Exotics, Aliens, and Outsiders*, ed. Marilyn Demarest and Toni Reed, 67–78. Westport, CT: Greenwood, 1999.

Hoeveler, Diane Long. "'A Draught of Sweet Poison': Food, Love, and Wounds" in *Jane Eyre* and *Villette*." *Prism(s): Essays in Romanticism* 7 (1999): 149–173.

Jacobus, Mary. "The Buried Letter: Feminism and Romanticism in *Villette*." In *Women Writing and Writing About Women*, ed. Mary Jacobus. London: Croom Helm, 1979.

Kavaler Adler, Susan. "Charlotte Brontë and the Feminine Self." *The American Journal of Psychoanalysis* 50:1 (March 1990): 37–43.

Matus, Jill L. "Looking at Cleopatra: The Expression and Exhibition of Desire in *Villette*." In *Victorian Literature and Culture*, ed. John Maynard and Adrienne Auslander Munich, 345–367. New York: AMS, 1993.

Nestor, Pauline (ed.) *Villette New Casebooks*. New York: St. Martin's, 1992.

Silver, Brenda R. "The Reflecting Reader in *Villette*." In *The Voyage In: Fictions of Female Development*, ed. Elizabeth Abel, Marianne Hirsch, and Elizabeth Langland, 90–111. Hanover, NH: University Press of New England, 1983.

Stewart, Garrett. "A Valediction For Bidding (*sic*) Mourning: Death and the Narratee in Brontë's *Villette*." In *Death & Representation*, ed. Sarah Webster Goodwin, 51–79. Baltimore: Johns Hopkins University Press, 1993.

Watkins, Susan. "Versions of the Feminine Subject in Charlotte Brontë's *Villette*." In *Ethics and the Subject*, ed. Karl Simms, 217–225. Amsterdam: Rodopi, 1997.

Wein, Toni. "Gothic Desire in Charlotte Brontë's *Villette*." *SEL: Studies in English Literature, 1500–1900*, 39:4 (autumn 1999): 733–746.

Wolstenholme, Susan. *Gothic (Re)Visions: Writing Women as Readers*. Albany: State University of New York Press, 1993.

THE PROFESSOR

Reviews

Blackburne. "*The Professor*." *Athenaeum*. June 13, 1857. 755–757.

Brontë, Charlotte. Preface to *The Professor*, 1851. *The Professor*, 1857. London: J. M. Dent & Sons, 1985.

"Currer Bell." *Blackwood's Edinburgh Magazine* 82 (501), July 1857. 77.

Criticism

Azim, Firdous. *The Colonial Rise of the Novel*. New York: Routledge, 1993.

Brown, Kate E. "Beloved Objects: Mourning, Materiality, and Charlotte Brontë's 'Never-Ending Story.'" *ELH (English Literary History)* 65:2 (Summer 1998): 395–421.

Federico, Annette R. "The Other Case: Gender and Narration in Charlotte Brontë's *The Professor*." *Papers on Language and Literature* 30:4 (fall 1994): 323–345.

Malone, Catherine. "'We Have Learnt to Love Her More than Her Books': The Critical Reception of Brontë's *Professor*." *Review of English Studies* 47:186 (May 1996): 175–187.

Wheeler, Michael D. "Literary and Biblical Allusion in *The Professor*." *Brontë Society Transactions* 17 (1976): 46–57.

CRITICAL STUDIES OF THE BRONTËS

Allott, Miriam, ed. *The Brontës, the Critical Heritage*. London, Boston: Routledge and Kegan Paul, 1974.

Beer, Patricia. *Reader, I Married Him: A Study of the Women Characters of Jane Austen, Charlotte Brontë, Elizabeth Gaskell, and George Eliot.* London: Macmillan, 1974.

Björk, Harriet. *The Language of Truth: Charlotte Brontë and the Woman Question.* Lund: Gleerup, 1974.

Boumelha, Penny. *Charlotte Brontë.* New York: Harvester/Wheatsheaf, 1990.

Burkhart, Charles. *Charlotte Brontë: A Psychosexual Study of Her Novels.* London: Victor Gollancz, 1973.

Chase, Karen. *Eros and Psyche: The Representation of Personality in Charlotte Brontë, Charles Dickens, and George Eliot.* New York and London: Methuen, 1984.

Davies, Stevie. *Emily Brontë: Heretic.* London: Women's Press, 1994.

Eagleton, Terry. *Myths of Power: A Marxist Study of the Brontës.* London: Macmillan, 1975.

Gates, Barbara Timm. *Critical Essays on Charlotte Brontë.* Boston: G. K. Hall, 1990.

Gilbert, Sandra M, and Susan Gubar. *The Madwoman in the Attic: The Woman Writer and the Nineteenth-Century Literary Imagination.* New Haven: Yale University Press, 1979.

Gordon, Felicia. *A Preface to the Brontës.* New York: Longman, 1989.

Gregor, Ian, ed. *The Brontës: A Collection of Critical Essays.* Englewood Cliffs, NJ: Prentice Hall, 1970.

Hewish, John. *Emily Brontë: A Critical and Biographical Study.* London: Macmillan, 1969.

Hoeveler, Diane Long. *Gothic Feminism: The Professionalization of Gender from Charlotte Smith to the Brontës.* University Park: Pennsylvania State University Press, 1999.

Imlay, Elizabeth. *Charlotte Brontë and the Mysteries of Love.* New York: St. Martin's, 1989.

Kaplan, Cora. *Sea Changes: Culture and Feminism.* London: Verso, 1986.

Keefe, Robert. *Charlotte Brontë's World of Death.* Austin: University of Texas Press, 1979.

Lloyd Evans, Barbara and Gareth. *The Scribner Companion to the Brontës.* New York: Scribner's, 1982.

Martin, Robert Bernard. *Charlotte Brontë's Novels: The Accents of Persuasion.* New York: Norton, 1966.

Maynard, John. *Charlotte Brontë and Sexuality.* Cambridge: Cambridge University Press, 1984.

McNees Eleanor, ed. *The Brontë Sisters: Critical Assessments.* East Sussex, England: Helm Information, 1996.

Moglen, Helen. *Charlotte Brontë: The Self Conceived.* New York: Norton, 1976.

Nestor, Pauline. *Charlotte Brontë.* New York: Macmillan, 1987.

O'Neill, Judith, ed. *Critics on Charlotte and Emily Brontë.* London: George Allen and Unwin, 1968.

Peters, Margot. *Charlotte Brontë: Style in the Novel.* Madison: University of Wisconsin Press, 1973.

Ratchford, Fanny Elizabeth. *The Brontës' Web of Childhood*. New York: Columbia University Press, 1941.

Showalter, Elaine. *A Literature of Their Own: British Women Novelists from Brontë to Lessing*. Princeton: Princeton University Press, 1977.

Shuttleworth, Sally. *Charlotte Brontë and Victorian Psychology*. Cambridge; New York: Cambridge University Press, 1996.

Stoneman, Patsy. *Brontë Transformations: the Cultural Dissemination of* Jane Eyre *and* Wuthering Heights. London; New York: Prentice Hall/Harvester Wheatsheaf, 1996.

Tayler, Irene. *Holy Ghosts: The Male Muses of Emily and Charlotte Brontë*. New York: Columbia University Press, 1990.

Thormrählen, Marianne. *The Brontës and Religion*. Cambridge, UK: Cambridge University Press, 2000.

Williams, Judith. *Perception and Expression in the Novels of Charlotte Brontë*. Ann Arbor and London: UMI Research Press, 1988.

Winnifrith, Tom. *The Brontës and Their Background: Romance and Reality*. New York: Barnes and Noble, 1973.

Wolstenholme, Susan. *Gothic (Re)Visions: Writing Women as Readers*. New York: State University of New York Press, 1993.

RELATED HISTORICAL AND SECONDARY SOURCES

Bersani, Leo. *A Future for Astyanax*. Boston: Little, Brown, 1969.

Ellis, Sarah Stickney. *The Wives of England, Their Relative Duties, Domestic Influence, and Social Obligations*. New York: J. & H. G. Langley, 1843.

Erickson, Carolly. *Our Tempestuous Day: A History of Regency England*. New York: William Morrow, 1986.

Fanon, Frantz. *The Wretched of the Earth*. Trans. Constance Farrington. New York: Grove Press, 1963.

————. *Black Skin, White Masks*. Trans. Charles L. Markmann. New York: Grove Press, 1967.

Hall, Calvin S., and Vernon J. Nordby. *A Primer of Jungian Psychology*. New York: Taplinger, 1973.

Jung, Carl Gustav. *Psyche and Symbol*. Ed. Violet S. de Laszlo. New York: Doubleday, 1958.

Lacan, Jacques. *Écrits: A Selection*. New York: Norton, 1977.

Newsome, David. *The Victorian World Picture*. New Brunswick, NJ: Rutgers University Press, 1997.

Patmore, Coventry. "The Rose of the World." In *Victorian Women: A Documentary Account of Women's Lives in Nineteenth-Century England, France, and the United States*, ed. Erna Olafson Hellerstein, Leslie Parker Hume, and Karen M. Offen, 134–140. Stanford: Stanford University Press, 1981.

Perkin, Joan. *Women and Marriage in Nineteenth-Century England*. London: Routledge, 1989.

Richter, David H. *The Critical Tradition: Classic Texts and Contemporary Trends.* New York: St. Martin's, 1989.

Said, Edward. *Orientalism.* London: Routledge, 1978.

Thompson, E. P. *The Making of the English Working Class.* New York: Random House, 1966.

Williams, Raymond. *The Long Revolution.* New York: Columbia University Press, 1972.

WEB SITES ON CHARLOTTE AND EMILY BRONTË

Brontë Parsonage Museum . Ed. The Brontë Society. 17 July 2000 <http://www.bronte.org.uk/>.

The Brontës and Phrenology. Ed. Peter Friesen. 1995–1997. Plattsburgh State University of New York. 8 August 2000 <http://www.plattsburgh.edu/faculty/friesep/index.htm>.

The Brontë Sisters Web. Ed. Mitsuharu Matsuoka. 26 June 2000. Nagoya University, Japan. 8 August 2000 <http://www.lang.nagoya-u.ac.jp/~matsuoka/Brontë.html>.

Brontë Society Website. Ed. Brontë Society. Brontë Parsonage Museum, Haworth, Keighley, West Yorkshire. 10 August 2000 <http://home.virtual-pc.com/bpmweb/>.

The Brontë Student Website. Ed. Brontë Society. 10 August 2000 <http://www.hevelius.demon.co.uk/bronte/>.

Emily Jane Brontë. Ed. Jody Allard. 10 August 2000 <http://www.geocities.com/CollegePark/1380/emily.htm>.

The Internet Library of Early Journals: A Digital Library of 18th and 19th Century Journals. Ed. Universities of Birmingham, Leeds, Manchester and Oxford. 14 August 2000 <http://www.bodley.ox.ac.uk/ilej/>.

Jack, A. A. "The Brontes: Bibliography." *The Cambridge History of English and American Literature in 18 Volumes* (1907–1921). Ed. A. W. Ward, A. R. Waller, W. P. Trent, J. Erskine, S. P. Sherman, and C. Van Doren. Vol. 13: *The Victorian Age.* Part One. Online edition published January 2000 by Bartleby.com. 4 December 2000. <http://www.bartleby.com/223/1200.html>.

The Romantic Chronology. Ed. Laura Mandell, Miami University of Ohio, and Alan Liu, University of California Santa Barbara. 10 August 2000 <http://www.qub.ac.uk/english/shuttle/rom-chrono/chrono.htm>.

Sublime Anxiety: The Gothic Family and the Outsider. Ed. Natalie Regensburg. 17 August 1999. University of Virginia. 10 August 2000 <http://www.lib.virginia.edu/exhibits/gothic/index.html>.

The Victorian Web. Ed. George P. Landow. 1985. Brown University. 10 August 2000 <http://www.stg.brown.edu/projects/hypertext/landow/victorian/victov.html>.

The Voice of the Shuttle. Ed. Alan Liu. University of California Santa Barbara. 10 August 2000 <http://vos.ucsb.edu/shuttle/english.html>.

Index

About the Author

BARBARA Z. THADEN is Assistant Professor of English at St. Augustine's College in Raleigh, NC. She has also taught high school English. She is the author of *The Maternal Voice in Victorian Fiction* (1997), *New Essays on the Maternal Voice in Victorian Fiction* (1995), and articles on Jane Austen, Dostoevsky, and others.